PROMOTING VALUES
DEVELOPMENT
IN COLLEGE
STUDENTS

Edited By

Jon C. Dalton
Acting Vice President for Student Affairs
Northern Illinois University

Volume 4; NASPA Monograph Series
Published by the National Association
of Student Personnel Administrators, Inc.

Library of Congress Cataloging-in-Publication Data
Main entry under title:
Promoting values development in college students.
    (NASPA monograph series; v. 4)
    Bibliography: p.
    1. College students—Conduct of life—Addresses, essay, lectures. 2. Moral development—Addresses, essay, lectures. 3. Moral education—Addresses, essays, lectures. 4. Values—Addresses, essay, lectures. I. Dalton, Jon C., 1941- . II. Series. BJ1661.P74   1985   174'.9379   85-24668
ISBN 0-931654-04-1

CONTENTS

Authors

Arthur Sandeen is Vice President for Student Affairs at the University of Florida. He is also Associate Professor of Higher Education at Florida.

Jon C. Dalton is Acting Vice President for Student Affairs at Northern Illinois University.

John M. Whiteley is Professor of Social Ecology and former Vice President for Student Affairs at the University of California, Irvine.

Barbara D. Bertin, Elizabeth A. Ferrant, and Norma Yokota are Research Associates in the Department of Social Ecology at the University of California, Irvine.

Margaret A. Healy is Coordinator of Research and Evaluation for Student Affairs at Iowa State University.

James E. Moore is Dean of Students at Marquette University.

James R. Rest is Professor of Educational Psychology at the University of Minnesota.

Martha McGinty Stodt is currently Adjunct Professor at Columbia University Graduate School of Business and former Associate Professor of Higher Education at Teachers College Columbia University.

James Thorius is Vice President for Student Affairs at Simpson College.

FOREWORD

Colleges and universities have, almost without exception, included a commitment to promote awareness and commitment to values as part of their educational mission. Today, as in the past, most colleges identify value development as one of their most important educational outcomes. Despite this commitment, however, one must search for examples of student development interventions designed specifically to promote values education in college students.

During the past decade, however, increasing attention has been given to examining the importance of value development in the higher education setting. Arthur Chickering, for example, has identified the development of integrity as one of the seven "vectors" of student development and concluded that the most significant contribution a college can make is to increase the role of values in the lives of students. John Whiteley's longitudinal study on character development among students in the Sierra Project at the University of California, Irvine, represents one of the most ambitious contemporary efforts to examine the development of moral reasoning in college students. The research efforts of Lawrence Kohlberg, William Perry, James Rest, and Marcia Mentkowski on moral development in college students are also widely known. Many student personnel professionals, however, are uncertain about practical ways to implement these research findings in student affairs programs and services. This monograph is dedicated to that purpose: to examine the significance of recent moral development theory and research for college student development and to demonstrate ways in which these findings can be incorporated into student affairs programs and services.

It will be useful for the reader to be familiar with the meaning of the following terms used in the monograph. "Values education" is an inclusive term used to refer to all educational efforts to enhance the role of values in the personal development of college students. "Moral development" is similar in meaning but used to refer more specifically to educational efforts to promote the development of ethical reasoning and understanding.

"Character education" is a traditional term broadly used to refer to the development of ethical conduct in students as well as ethical reasoning and understanding. The differences in emphasis of these terms are not important for the purposes of this monograph. We will use all three terms to refer to educational efforts to enhance ethical reasoning and conduct among college students.

Although the monograph includes some review and discussion of research and theory in values development, it is written primarily for student personnel practitioners. Most of the authors are student affairs professionals who have struggled themselves with the complexity of promoting values education in student personnel practice. Hopefully, our attempt to apply research and theory on values education to college student development will be useful to our student personnel colleagues who are already actively involved in values education efforts. It may also enable those who claim to be value-neutral to resolve the inexorable moral dilemmas confronted in college student personnel work.

Finally, we wish to express much appreciation to Martha Stodt, Editor of the NASPA Monograph Board, for her helpfulness and contributions to this monograph. We are indebted, as well, to Lorene Burger and Dale Parkhouse for their considerable assistance in preparing the manuscript.

CHAPTER ONE

The Legacy of Values Education in College Student Personnel Work

by Arthur Sandeen

In 1636, the original statutes of Harvard College stated:

> Everyone shall consider the main End of his life and studies, to know God and Jesus Christ which is eternal life . . . they shall eschew all profanation of God's holy name, attributes, word, ordinances, and times of worship, and study with reverence and love carefully to retain God and His truth in their minds.

Over 300 years later, the stated purposes of the newly founded University of North Florida included the following:

> The University's primary responsibility is to serve the Northeast Florida area by providing a sound foundation in professional education, to meet local needs in business administration, to reflect the economic characteristics of the community, and to prepare students for useful careers (1978).

The dramatic differences in these two statements of purpose reflect the development of higher education in the United States. When colleges only served a select few, there was little question about the place of values. The primary reason for the college's existence was to assure correct moral behavior in its students, most of whom were very young boys preparing for the clergy. But now there are over 3000 different "post-secondary institutions" and they serve a great variety of purposes and a wide diversity of students. The specialization of knowledge, emphasis upon research, extension and vocational preparation have all changed the nature of higher education, and challenged its role in promoting value development in students.

This is not to suggest that American higher education has abandoned its interest in teaching values to its students. Colleges and universities in this country are still striving to combine the best aspects of the English and German traditions which reflect their values and heritage. During the great student turmoil of the 1960s colleges and society were essentially forced into a confrontation of values that reflected the contrasts between two traditions. The commitment to scholarship, to vocational and professional preparation, and to research were, by then, values which were firmly and permanently entrenched as the dominant purposes of higher education. But when students challenged these values in ways that upset the academy and society, the public clearly indicated that colleges were somehow responsible for the behavior of students and should have taught them appropriate values.

Whether values are taught formally in the curriculum or not, the attitudes, conduct, and beliefs of students have always been influenced by their colleges. The specific organization of knowledge, the academic requirements set forth in the catalog, the manner in which the faculty relate to the students, the role accorded to out-of-class experiences, the emphasis given to policies and procedures, and the standards set for admission and graduation all reveal certain values of the college, and their expectations for values development in students.

With the emergence of the University (as opposed to the old college) in this century, with its emphasis upon research and scholarship, the concept of "ethical neutrality" appeared, and faculty often assumed that the value development of their students was something for which they no longer had (or wanted) any responsibility. If the purpose of the University was to be the advancement of knowledge, then the emphasis must be firmly upon the academic disciplines and subject matter specialities that will produce that knowledge. The role of the faculty changed dramatically, and the new professional scholars used their academic freedom to pursue their disciplines. This shift was a reflection of the University's desire and need to participate in the rapidly developing industrial and economic revolution of the time. It changed for all time the relationship of faculty to students, and thus, the nature of the institution. The primary role of the professor was now scholarship, and not the moral development of the students. This change, of course, resulted in what is now student personnel administration. If the faculty no longer were to assume responsibility for the personal lives of students, who should? In 1890, colleges were clearly not willing to abandon this task, nor were their benefactors or the parents of the students willing to allow them to do so. The German influence upon scholarship and research had taken over, but not to the exclusion of the English tradition of educating the whole person. A new office was to be created to carry out this historical English mission, and a member of the faculty was usually asked by the President to assume this position. The beginnings of the student affairs profession were thus established. From its inception, therefore, the student affairs profession has had significant responsibility for the values education of college students.

When LeBaron Russell Briggs was appointed dean at Harvard in 1890, there was no job description, and very little direction was given to him by the President or the faculty. But there was little doubt about the values his office represented. In an atmosphere of increasing specialization and scholarship, Dean Briggs' role was to maintain collegiate and human ideals. He represented the values that old Harvard wanted to develop in its students—good manners, honesty, a sense of fairness and respect, and personal conscience. Indeed, it was clear at that time that Deans were selected because they epitomized these traits themselves. Thus, their role was somehow to transmit these values to their students. There is considerable evidence to indicate that their influence was substantial in this regard:

For every sort of man, Dean Briggs was a cheerful, hopeful, friend; but the underdog, the man to whom being down and out was a grave possibility, seemed to be the object of his most ardent, most affectionate concern. If all the records of his encouragement to struggling college men could be brought together, they would make such a volume as has never been written. So acute were his powers of observation that students used to declare he would recognize a hungry man clear across the College Yard. Somehow all the men who were working their way through college seemed to be known to him, and he constantly kept an eye out for their comfort (Brown, 1926).

If these early deans succeeded, it was largely due to their personal charisma or courageous persistence. Enrollments were small, so it was still possible for the deans to know many, if not all, of the undergraduates. This enabled them to exert their influence on the lives of students in direct and personal ways. It was not unusual in 1910 for a Dean to be a counselor, confidant of the family, loan agent, enforcer of policies, academic advisor, visitor to the sick, and "conscience of the campus." The early leaders in the student affairs profession exerted their influence upon student values by example and force of personality rather than through any organized program of activities or set of policies. There was little debate about whether the college should attempt to transmit values—this was an expectation that was clear—and the dean was the primary vehicle through which this was to be accomplished.

From its informal beginnings to the highly specialized present, the student affairs profession has, in effect, operated at cross-purposes with faculty values. The efforts to establish support programs for students and to actively promote values education have often been viewed with disdain by some faculty and with indifference by many others. This is because the ideas and programs advanced by student affairs personnel essentially have represented a set of educational values and philosophy that have conflicted with those of the faculty. The most successful student affairs deans, from 1890 to the present, are those who have been able to win the support (or at least the acquiescence) of the faculty without compromising their own commitments to value development in students.

It was not long after the emergence of the early deans that they began taking advantage of the considerable assistance becoming available in the psychological and mental health movements. The new emphasis upon individual differences and the "scientific study of the student" (Harper, 1899) gave encouragement especially to student affairs personnel because it provided a means by which to better assist students in their overall personal and moral development. There was excitement about psychology and testing, and many student affairs deans seized this opportunity to expand their institution's commitment to student concerns related to values and ethical issues. Tools were now available that could aid the college in learning more about students, what their interests and problems were, and what their personal, social, and ethical concerns might be. The student affairs deans argued that such efforts deserved institutional support because they would enable the college to have a more positive impact upon the lives of students and lead to better decisions in admissions and course selection. It was no longer a sign of moral weakness to reveal psychological or physical health problems, and, in fact, the professional treatment of them might aid in academic and personal growth.

At the same time, coeducation, larger enrollments, and the emergence of student organizations and athletics caused colleges and universities to provide supervision for these activities. Students spent many hours in these activities and most colleges recognized that they would require careful monitoring if the "right" student values were to emerge. Woodrow Wilson recognized this at Princeton when he argued that:

> So long as instruction and life do not emerge in our colleges, so long as what the undergraduates do and what they are taught occupy two separate airtight compartments in their consciousness, so long will the college be ineffectual (Wilson, 1925).

Thus, another important function was assumed by the early student affairs deans—that of the supervision of student activities. Concern about student values was clearly reflected in the assumption of these responsibilities by the college. If student organizations were to function effectively, there must be freedom of association, respect for diversity of opinion and action, trust in the handling of money, and personal accountability for one's action. With coeducation, there was to be supervision of social activities to insure that the current values of society were upheld by the college. These rather considerable tasks became part of the student affairs program, and, of course, remain to this day.

Within 35 years of the appointment of Dean Briggs at Harvard, the three major professional associations in student affairs were founded. The National Association of Women's Deans was organized in 1916, the National Association of Deans of Men in 1919, and the National Association of Personnel and Placement Officers (later ACPA) in 1924. These organizations, together with the establishment of the first formal Department of Student Personnel in 1919 at Northwestern, led to the rapid expansion of this young movement. The importance of values or "character" development in college students was a central concern of these developing professional groups.

When Robert Clothier of the University of Pittsburgh spoke as Chairman of a national committee on "Principles and Functions of College Personnel Work" in 1931, the value implications were clear:

> Personnel work in a college or university is the systematic bringing to bear on the individual student all those influences, of whatever nature, which will stimulate him and assist him, through his own efforts to develop in body, mind, and character to the limit of his individual capacity for growth, and helping him to apply his powers so developed most effectively to the work of the world.

The principles and functions in the Clothier Report stressed a relatively passive, services approach for student affairs, and the primary values implied were (1) taking into account individual differences among students, (2) minimizing student academic failure, and (3) preparing students to be as marketable as possible after graduation. The Clothier Report did, however, stress the continued importance of ethical development in college students as a central objective of student affairs work. The faculty values which dominated higher education resulted in a rather passive administrative role for these deans, and much of their work was directed at assisting individual students with their academic, personal, and social adjustment to the existing campus community. A proactive or teaching role for the student personnel movement had not yet emerged.

In 1937, the "Student Personnel Point of View" was published under the leadership the American Council of Education. This important document was used extensively by colleges and universities in the development of additional student affairs programs for students. It was very similar in content and emphasis to the Clothier Report issued several years earlier. A long list of student problems and needs was matched with a set of services designed to address them. For student affairs staff, the same value orientation remained—the role of student affairs was to help students in their personal adjustment to the campus environment and to promote the awareness and development necessary to prepare students for the world of work.

Student affairs deans spoke often to each other, but infrequently to their faculty colleagues, whose priorities remained almost exclusively on values represented by scholarship and academic disciplines. Thus, it was not surprising when W. H. Cowley, speaking at the 19th annual conference of NASPA in 1937 in Austin, Texas, listed among the 22 major activities of the student affairs field the following:

> 22. Educating the faculty and administrative officers
> to the importance of the personnel point of view and
> of personnel services.

The primary values of the institution remained elsewhere, and the student affairs function continued to represent a minority set of educational values on the campus. The deans had real concern for the moral development of the student, but often they assumed their formal responsibility alone. The need to promote broader awareness and acceptance of student development activities with faculty became an important objective of student affairs deans.

The growing professionalism of student affairs was reflected in the work of the Committee on Student Personnel Work of the American Council on Education, chaired for many years by E. G. Williamson of the University of Minnesota. This committee appointed a special group to recommend policies and practices that would enable student personnel deans to adapt to the special needs of students following World War II. The report, issued in 1945, was entitled "Student Personnel Work in the Post-war College," and the Commission chairman was Willard Blaesser. This remarkable document made recommendations in virtually every area of student affairs, and the overwhelming emphasis was upon the need to assist students in all aspects of their adjustment to college.

All of these developments were extensions of the basic commitment to the moral education of the student that has been a part of college personnel work from its beginnings. With expanded enrollments and older students, it was essential to provide housing, counseling, and recreation, but these were essentially means to a greater end, and that was the enhancement of the students' life, in all its dimensions. When deans described their work to outsiders or to their colleagues, the emphasis was always upon the lives of students, and how the deans wanted to develop them to become better persons.

Student affairs deans, aware of the changes taking place in society and on the campus, reconvened the American Council on Education's Committee on Student Personnel Work in June of 1949 to revise the original Student Personnel Point of View Report. Again chaired by E. G. Williamson, the 1949 report set out three new goals, significant in that they represented a set of new values to be addressed by the student affairs field:

1. Education for a fuller realization of democracy in every phase of living;

2. Education directly and explicitly for international understanding and cooperation;

3. Education for the application of creative imagination and trained intelligence to the solution of social problems and to the administration of public affairs.

While the emphasis of this revised document was on successful adjustment to the college, it identified several value outcomes which were indispensable to education. The report included sections on helping students achieve ethical meaning in life, how to learn to live effectively with others, and how to progress toward satisfying sexual adjustments. Thus, the report continued the long tradition in student affairs of seeking ways to integrate value education as part of the broader education mission of the college.

These significant changes, of course, were a reflection of the social and economic changes that occurred after World War II. Society's new emphasis on the values of equal access, social integration, and freedom of choice would open new opportunities to the student affairs profession, and would change much of its emphasis. This changing emphasis reflected a maturing and more confident profession, willing to speak out on social and educational issues. Thus, in 1957 E. G. Williamson wrote a very influential article in the Educational Record titled "The Dean of Students as Educator." In it, he stated:

> While we clearly recognize the value of the formal education which takes place when student and teacher communicate directly in the classroom, laboratory, or office, we need not conclude that these are the only important loci of instruction.

Williamson described the programs instituted at Minnesota regarding student participation in University affairs, and the resolution of social conflicts. In each activity, student affairs staff served as teachers to the students, and were clearly committed to promoting certain values in their work with students such as: group cooperation; consideration of a diversity of viewpoints; a rational approach to decision making; and above all, respect for individual dignity. These values were important not only for the campus where diversity was increasing but also for responsible citizenship in society where profound issues of social justice were being addressed.

Of course, the turmoil in civil rights in the country presented new opportunities for student affairs staff to help students deal with important value questions. Many deans were forceful leaders for their institutions on the issues of racial integration and equal access during the late 1950s and early 1960s. It was most often the student affairs staff that organized seminars, debates, retreats, colloquia, and cross-cultural workshops designed to teach students about such values as tolerance, mutual respect, equal access, and even love. The dean was frequently the central campus and community figure in providing the leadership on these important issues, and these issues provided the sufficient stimulus for the profession as a whole to take the offensive.

The civil rights movement also resulted in a changed relationship between the student and the institution, and it was very difficult for many faculty, parents, board members, and presidents to accept the reality that students were legal adults and had the same constitutional rights as other citizens. On virtually every campus, standards of due process in the handling of student disciplinary cases were established and formalized, and the student affairs staff provided the leadership. For students, the values being advocated by their deans were clear—fairness, openness, and equality. Such activity by student affairs staff placed them in a new leadership role on the campus.

During the 1960s and early 1970s, of course, the college campuses became the primary place where the nation's anguish regarding racial inequality and the Vietnam War would be expressed. Never in the history of the profession had the emotional and professional maturity of student affairs staff been tested to the degree they were during this period. For some, the emotional costs were too high and they left the profession. The frustration, anger, bitterness, violence, and distrust experienced by students was a constant reality, and some student affairs staff simply chose not to deal with it. For most, however, it was a period when the most vigorous and mature leadership regarding human values was needed and the dean was usually the central campus figure in this effort. Many of the most fundamental human values were being threatened—freedom of expression, respect for diversity, honesty, and respect for property. Student affairs staff everywhere spent long days and nights teaching students about these values by personal example, conflict resolution, introducing new policies, and intervening with campus and state authorities.

The profession itself understood the nature of the campus turmoil, and initiated and implemented one of the most influential documents in its history: *The Joint Statement of Rights and Freedoms of Students* (American Association of University Professors, 1967). This document set forth the essential conditions for student freedom, access, due process, and open expression, and served as a model for scores of campuses. It also enabled the student affairs dean to assume a leadership role on the campus and to demonstrate in real ways a commitment to certain educational and human values. The Joint Statement was accomplished through the collaboration of 10 national professional associations, and this experience encouraged deans on many campuses to initiate similar collaborative efforts with academic departments, student groups, and even community organizations. Student affairs staff were still engaged in the important tasks of assisting students in their academic, personal, financial, and social adjustment to the college, but events of the 1960s and early 1970s thrust them into new, proactive leadership roles on their campuses. In effect, student affairs deans at many institutions now had a clear idea of what it was they intended to teach through their own "curriculum," and, most importantly, they had now gained the confidence and the stature to do it.

The work of student affairs leaders during this time was greatly assisted by the significant amount of excellent research and writing in higher education, psychology, and sociology. Prominent among the contributors were Pace and Stern (1958), Eddy (1959), Sanford (1968), Katz (1969), Chickering (1969), Brown (1972), Cross (1972), the Carnegie Commission on Higher Education (1973), and Astin (1978). Robert Brown's work on *Tomorrow's Higher Education* (THE) project and Arthur Chickering's work titled *Education and Identity* are of special note, because they illustrate the important changes that had taken place in the role of student affairs professionals. Brown argued that student affairs staff must recognize that student development is a total campus effort, and that direct ties with the faculty must be established to support a concern for both affective and cognitive student development. Chickering's research identified various "vectors" of student development, and suggested specific educational activities and residential arrangements that might enhance that development. Student affairs leaders were now spending their time organizing various learning activities to achieve specific behavioral outcomes in students. The concern to address student values development, present since the beginnings of the profession, was there again, and new and more organized ways to enhance this development were taking place.

Undoubtedly the greatest advances in assisting college students with their ethical and moral development have taken place in the past 20 years. Important theoretical contributions have been made, especially by Kohlberg (1971) and Perry (1970). They provided the background and foundation for student affairs leaders to use in designing programs and activities for students that might assist them in becoming more aware of and clarifying their value positions. The role of the student affairs staff member was again that of a proactive teacher.

The 1980s find student affairs leaders engaged in a wider variety of responsibilities than ever before. The large numbers of adult and part-time students, the current preoccupation with career preparation, the increasing competition for students, and reduced budgets have all presented new challenges to the profession. The concern with student value development remains a central one with most student affairs staff. Delworth and Hanson (1980), Knefelkamp (1978), and Chickering (1981) have provided new insights and research that can assist students in their moral and ethical growth through developmental instruction and further collaboration with academic departments. Reflecting the increased expertise and independence of the profession, some student affairs staff now are conducting specific value clarification and development programs, and are attracting private funding for their efforts. However, Frederick Rudolf (1977) warns that "recent efforts to develop specific courses in values have a synthetic quality about them: Unless the entire institutional environment is recognized as making conscious and unconscious statements of value, value courses as such run the risk of being quaint and strangely and unintentionally irrelevant." Thus, the tension between the dominant intellectual emphasis of most faculty and the human development emphasis of student affairs continues to this day. There are significant, well organized and collaborative efforts now on many campuses designed to help students learn more about their own values, and to develop a keener awareness of value implications. Most often, such efforts have been initiated, organized, and implemented by student affairs staff. These efforts, while laudable, are still overshadowed by higher education's current emphasis upon vocational preparation and academic discipline.

The student affairs profession was born in the nineteenth century primarily as a result of a shift of emphasis in educational values. From the beginning, student affairs represented an institutional attempt to retain at least a modicum of commitment to the development of human beings at a time when academic and intellectual values had come to dominate the scene. The early leaders in the profession struggled against very difficult odds to establish a humane atmosphere on campus to provide ethical development and to personalize the educational experience for students. This struggle and conflict has continued throughout this century, and the student affairs personnel made important advances during the period 1920-50 in expanding the profession and in extending the various services. They were also at odds with the dominant values of their institutions, and established student affairs programs whose purpose was to accommodate to the institution as they found it, and to assist students in their overall academic and personal adjustment to the college. The past 30 years has seen some exciting new developments within student affairs, as it has gained more maturity as a profession, taking responsibility for its own growth and programs. Virtually all of the activities carried on by student affairs staff are value oriented. This value orientation is seen in admissions, orientation, financial aid, student activities, campus discipline, housing, student health, counseling, career planning, and placement. Beyond these essential services, student affairs staff now are conducting sophisticated programs specifically designed to assist students confront, clarify, and become more aware of their own value orientations. Such efforts are consistent with the origins and purposes of the profession itself, and while they are still dominated by the overwhelming emphasis of the institution upon academic and vocational values, they represent a significant advancement in student affairs' historic efforts to address human values.

References

American Association of University Professors. (1969). Joint statement on rights and freedoms of students. McJoughin, L. (Ed.) *Academic freedom and tenure*. Madison, Wisconsin: University of Wisconsin Press.

Astin, A. W. (1978). *Four critical years*. San Francisco: Jossey-Bass.

Brown, R. D. (1972). *Student development in tomorrow's higher education—A return to the academy*. Washington, D.C.: American Personnel and Guidance Association.

Brown, R. W. (1926). *Dean Briggs* (p. 131). New York: Harper & Brothers.

Carnegie Commission on Higher Education. (1973). *Priorities for action*. New York: McGraw-Hill.

Chickering, A. W. (1969). *Education and identity*. San Francisco: Jossey-Bass.

Chickering, A. W. (1981). *The modern American college*. San Francisco: Jossey-Bass.

Clothier, R. C. (June 1931). College personnel principles and functions. *Personnel journal*, 10, #1, p. 10.

Cowley, W. H. (April 2, 1937). The disappearing dean of men. Address presented at the nineteenth annual conference of the national association of deans and advisers of men. Austin, Texas.

Cross, K. P. (1972). *Beyond the open door*. San Francisco: Jossey-Bass.

Delworth, U. & Hanson, G. R. (1980). *Student services: A handbook for the profession*. San Francisco: Jossey-Bass.

Eddy, E. D. (1959). *The college influence on student character*. Washington, D. C.: American Council on Education.

Harper, W. R. (1899). The scientific study of the student. In *The trend in higher education* (pp. 317-326). Chicago: University of Chicago Press.

Institution role and scope of Florida's public universities. (1978). State University System of Florida Publication. Tallahassee. p. 40.

Katz, J. (1969). *No time for youth*. San Francisco: Jossey-Bass.

Knefelkamp, L. L., Widick, C., & Parker, C. A. (eds.) (1978). *New directions for student services; Applying new developmental findings*, 4. San Francisco: Jossey-Bass.

Kohlberg, L. (1971). Stages of moral development. In Beck, C. M., Crittenden, B. S., & Sullivan, E. V. (Eds.). *Moral education*. Toronto: University of Toronto Press.

Pace, C. R. & Stern, G. G. (1958). An approach to the measurement of psychological characteristics of college environments. *Journal of educational psychology*, 49, 5, pp. 269-277.

Perry, W., Jr. (1970). *Forms of intellectual and ethical development in the college years: A scheme*. New York: Holt, Rinehart, and Winston.

Rudolph, F. (1977). *Curriculum: A history of the American undergraduate course of study since 1636* (p. 288). San Francisco: Jossey-Bass.

Sanford, N. (1968). *Where colleges fail*. San Francisco: Jossey-Bass.

The student personnel point of view. (1937, June). *A report of a conference on the philosophy and development of student personnel work in college and university*. American Council on Education Studies, Ser. 1, Vol. 1, no. 3. Washington, D. C.: American Council on Education.

Williamson, E. G. (1949). *The student personnel point of view*. American Council on Education Studies, Series VI, Student Personnel Work, No. 13. Washington, D. C.: American Council on Education.

Williamson, E. G. (July, 1957). The dean of students as educator. *The educational record*, 36, pp. 230-240.

Wilson, W. (1925). The spirit of learning. *Selected literacy and political papers and addresses of Woodrow Wilson* (p. 244). New York: Grosset and Dunlap.

CHAPTER TWO

Values Education: A New Priority for College Student Development

by Jon C. Dalton

One of the reasons student affairs staff have renewed their interest and involvement in values education is because of widespread concern about the erosion of ethical values in college students. Recent research on the changing attitudes and values of college students has revealed some disturbing findings. In the past ten years a virtual revolution in college student beliefs and values has occurred. Alexander Astin's (1977) longitudinal research on college student characteristics indicates a trend of increasing materialism and hedonism and a corresponding decline in altruism and social consciousness. His student profile data collected each year on thousands of graduating high school seniors confirm a moral malaise among the young in which concern for status, self-fulfillment, and money have overshadowed concern about the welfare of other people, for human service, and the needs of society. The resulting "privatism" or moral passivity in college student values and conduct runs counter to many of the student development outcomes actively promoted by student affairs professionals.

Arthur Levine's (1980) Carnegie Foundation studies support Astin's general assessment of contemporary college student values. Levine argues that disillusionment with society's values and institutions as well as fear of the future have caused college students to become morally cynical and self-centered. He characterized the contemporary moral outlook of college students as a "Titanic ethic" or "meism" in which values are self-centered. In such a value system there is little place for altruism or other forms of moral obligation and responsibility that have traditionally been defined as integral to moral character. Levine's description may be overstated; there are too many examples of morally committed students to conclude that this college generation is simply hedonistic. And yet, even the casual observer can see that there is a new materialism and self-indulgence on campus.

Moreover, these changes in student values have occurred during a period in which there has been a significant increase in problems with the ethical conduct of college students. Some recent studies (Carnegie Council, 1979) have shown an alarming increase in cheating on campus as well as an acceptance of cheating behavior. The author's (Barnett and Dalton, 1981) research on cheating indicates that college faculty and staff generally see only the tip of the iceberg when it comes to academic dishonesty. Indeed, some studies have shown that many of our best students now feel that cheating is necessary in order to keep their competitive edge.

Concern about cheating, however, goes beyond the conduct of college students. There is some evidence that the current moral malaise of college students is, in part, a reflection of the neglect of ethical values and standards in the institutional life of colleges and universities. The Carnegie Commission (1979) found in a national study of higher education institutions that cheating was common in everything from faculty plagiarism to false advertising in college catalogues. Abuse in college athletics typically gets the major public attention but the Commission concluded that there are serious ethical problems in many areas of higher education. These problems impact on the moral development of college students because their values are greatly influenced by the moral standards and conduct of faculty and staff with whom they interact and typically view as authority figures.

The Hastings Center (1980) found in its research on the teaching of ethics in colleges and universities that not much was happening, or to use the words of the Center report, "There is in higher education a sense of moral drift, of ethical uncertainty, and a withering away of some traditional roots and moorings" (p. 2). Almost universally, colleges declare their commitment to values education in catalogues and convocations but, according to the Hastings Center Report, little is specifically provided in the curriculum or extracurriculum to *intentionally* promote this development in students. To the contrary, the study found that courses in the humanities and liberal arts had been dropped in significant numbers over the past several years in order to make room for courses in professional and technical curriculae.

Concern about value issues is also reflected in the questions and problems identified by college students themselves. These questions and problems reveal the fact that students are perplexed about the complex moral issues of their day. There have been few historical periods which have generated such profound moral dilemmas for youth as the latter half of the twentieth century. Richard Morrill (1980) claims that students face a time of critical issues, and intractable problems in which they must make very tough moral choices. Unfortunately, college students often get little assistance from colleges and universities in confronting such issues and learning how to make such moral choices. Despite the widespread concern about values education, there is still considerable uncertainty and disagreement among student affairs staff about how to best promote it. They continue to give lip service to the importance of value development in college students but, since the 1960s, have been much more reluctant to actively promote this development. Their reluctance is part of a broader retreat from values education which some say has affected all of higher education. Morrill (1980) argues that the campus has turned away from meddling and moralizing, but has not found credible and effective ways to meet its expressed commitment to students as persons. Hall (1979) concludes that colleges and universities take a *laissez faire* attitude toward moral education. Such an approach keeps educators from dealing effectively with the moral domain and fosters the impression that anything more than merely mentioning values is forbidden. Many other leading educators (e.g. Bok, 1976; Brown and Canon, 1978; and McBee, 1982) have expressed concern about the neglect of values education in higher education.

The uncertainty about how to approach values education has persuaded many student affairs staff to adopt a "values neutral" position. Since the 1960s discipline, control, and values training by student personnel staff have been greatly reduced or dropped altogether. Student values have come to be viewed as private matters which fall outside the purview of the college. Since student values are now regarded as largely private, personal matters, it follows logically that many student personnel workers believe they should take a non-directive role in their working relationships with students and assume a value neutral stance. To them "value neutral" means that staff should *avoid* transmitting or endorsing any particular set of moral values or beliefs. This approach is almost the reverse of the traditional character development philosophy. There is no doubt that value neutrality has helped to solve the problems of indoctrination and conformity and is more compatible with the new student body which is increasingly diverse and pluralistic. The new value neutrality approach has become the dominating credo in student personnel practice. This approach has, however, presented serious problems for many student affairs staff who also feel that values education is an important student development priority.

Why is value neutrality a problem? One reason is that student affairs staff generally recognize that they are unavoidably involved in values education; it comes with the territory. Despite their claim to be neutral, student affairs staff find themselves promoting values through rules, regulations, and role modeling. They continue to admonish students not to cheat, steal, discriminate, haze, or drink excessively. While student personnel staff publicly declare that they are neutral about values, they find in the practice of their work with students that they cannot be neutral.

Another reason value neutrality is a problem is that it is a principle which seems impossible to apply in our work with students. Whether it is dealing with a serious student conduct problem, resolving a cheating incident, deciding on birth control and abortion services in the health service, or counseling a student who has contemplated suicide, one quickly recognizes that it is impossible to be neutral about the important value issues at stake. One may start off with a neutral position on the values implicit in the situation, but eventually one gets to the unavoidable point of helping students to struggle with issues of responsibility, consideration, and fairness. This encounter involves implicit considerations and decisions about values. It is a role and responsibility which is at the heart of the professional work of college student personnel staff. Even though one might like to remain neutral, circumstances seldom permit that luxury.

Steven Muller (1982), president of Johns Hopkins University, recently discussed how universities are turning out what he called "highly skilled barbarians." Muller claims that the biggest downfall in higher education today is that college staff and faculty fail to expose students to values. "We really don't provide a value framework to young people who more and more are searching for it," Muller argues (p. 3). He noted that universities are turning out people who are very expert in the laboratory, or at the computer, or in surgery, or in the law courts, but who have no real understanding of the moral obligations of their own society. It is a remarkable statement of advocacy of values education from the president of one of the nation's leading research universities.

Like Muller, Arthur Chickering (1969) argues in *Education and Identity* that educators must help students not only to clarify their values but also to humanize them. Educators are needed to help students examine their ethical obligations to other people, to the environment, to their profession. Chickering concludes his book by claiming that the greatest contribution a college can make is to increase the role of values in their lives of students.

Clearly, there is a new priority for values education today. It is a priority deeply rooted in the legacy of student personnel work but felt today with a new sense of urgency. The priority is for a more proactive position with respect to values education and moral development as important objectives of college student development. Until the last decade student affairs staff have been justifiably concerned about the lack of a sound theoretical base for approaching values development in college students. An important factor in alleviating this concern has been the considerable research on moral development by Lawrence Kohlberg (1969, 1973, 1979), William Perry (1970), Tom Lickona (1976), Carol Gilligan (1982) and others. These researchers have provided an important new literature on how moral reasoning and ethical development occurs. Student personnel professionals now have a much better empirical base from which to approach values development in college students than perhaps at any time in their history. Today, there is probably more active research and publication on moral development than any other area of college student development. Much work needs to be done, however, in exploring the practical applications of that theory and research for student personnel practice.

Values education is by no means a new area of intervention for student affairs staff. Despite the popularity of value neutrality, student affairs staff are frequently involved in sponsoring activities designed to promote awareness and development of values in students. In order to learn more about the actual programming strategies which were used by student affairs staff in promoting values education, Dalton, Barnett, and Healey (1982) surveyed over 1000 NASPA chief student personnel administrators. These student affairs leaders were asked to identify the activities sponsored by their division which were intended to help promote values education. The following activities were mentioned most frequently:

Table 1
Activities Used for Values
Education Interventions

Activity	Total		Public		Religious		Private	
	N	%	N	%	N	%	N	%
1. Alcohol Education	72	12	45	12	14	11	13	12
2. Values clarification	68	11	39	11	15	12	14	14
3. Judicial boards	56	9	33	9	12	9	11	10
4. Leadership training	52	10	41	11	4	3	7	6
5. Faith development	50	8	16	4	24	18	10	9
6. Human Relations	39	6	22	6	9	7	8	7
7. Orientation	34	5	20	5	8	6	6	5
8. Volunteer projects	26	4	16	4	6	5	4	4
9. Career Development	27	5	17	5	5	4	5	5
10. Sexuality programs	25	5	18	5	4	3	3	3
11. Contemporary issues	23	3	12	3	6	5	5	5
12. Other activities	151	22	97	25	24	17	30	20
	623	100	376	100	131	100	116	100

The survey responses revealed that a wide variety of activities are used as a means to help students think and act ethically. The variety of activities suggest that values are regarded as an important dimension of many student development interventions. Moreover, there were few significant differences among staff in public, private, and religious colleges and universities in the activities they used for values education interventions. Staff in public institutions used leadership activities more frequently than did staff in other types of institutions while staff in religious institutions used faith development activities more often to promote values education.

When the student affairs leaders were asked what value issues they most frequently sought to address in their values education activities they identified the following:

Table 2
Value Issues

Issues	X	N	%
1. Irresponsible behavior	623	336	54
2. Interpersonal conflicts	623	318	51
3. Disrespect of others	623	249	40
4. Alcohol/Drug abuse	623	202	32
5. Prejudice	623	182	29
6. Health/Wellness	623	168	27
7. Academic Dishonesty	623	141	23
8. Sexism	623	140	23
9. Racism	623	136	22
10. Sexual behavior	623	129	21

It is interesting to note that four of the issues (disrespect of others, prejudice, sexism, racism) reflect concern on the part of respondents with students' social attitudes and treatment of others. Over half the respondents identified interpersonal conflicts as their most serious student conduct issue.

Finally, the student affairs leaders were asked to identify the most important values they sought to promote in values education activities.

The values mentioned most frequently are listed below:

Table 3
Values Promoted in Educational Activities

Activity	%	Activity	%
Alcohol Education		*Values Clarification*	
1. Responsibility for self	86	1. Self awareness	69
2. Self Awareness	67	2. Responsibility for self	50
3. Self discipline	56	3. Understanding others	46
4. Respect for others	43	4. Respect for others	32
5. Helping Others	24	5. Individual effort	13
Leadership Training		*Judicial Board Training*	
1. Cooperation	72	1. Fairness	65
2. Understanding others	43	2. Honesty	49
3. Self awareness	36	3. Respect for others	47
4. Assertiveness	26	4. Responsibility for self 47	
5. Helping others	25	5. Self discipline	33
Faith Development		*Human Relations*	
1. Religious belief	86	1. Respect for others	77
2. Respect for others	34	2. Understanding others	67
3. Helping others	26	3. Self awareness	51
4. Self awareness	26	4. Tolerance	49
5. Responsibility for self	26	5. Cooperation	13
Orientation		*Volunteer Projects*	
1. Responsibility for self	75	1. Helping others	89
2. Self awareness	44	2. Understanding others	70
3. Cooperation	37	3. Respect for others	41
4. Respect for others	28	4. Self awareness	36
Career Development		*Sexuality*	
1. Self awareness	78	1. Self awareness	73
2. Responsibility for self	74	2. Responsibility for self	68
3. Independence	30	3. Respect for others	48
4. Individual effort	30	4. Assertiveness	36
5. Assertiveness	26	5. Understanding others	32

The popularity of these values among student personnel leaders suggests that they may constitute a set of "core values" which are regarded as essential in the values education of college students. It is evident from this survey that college student personnel staff are actively involved in values education activities despite the popularity of the value neutral approach. They are clearly involved in helping students to clarify values as well as promoting particular core values which are regarded as indispensable to education and student development.

Student affairs staff are perhaps in the most strategic position on campus to help students explore and discuss ethical issues. No one else touches students in so many areas of their lives as college student affairs staff do. No one else on campus has so many natural opportunities to promote awareness and consideration of ethical issues with college students and to assist them in the process of developing values. In view of the increasing urgency of ethical issues and problems which confront students, it is important that student affairs staff take a more formal and active role in promoting values education as part of their student development efforts.

As Art Sandeen has shown in Chapter One, the concern for values development in students has always been a part of the mission of American higher education and one of the earliest roles which shaped the student affairs profession. It is a role which has undergone considerable reexamination and reformulation but which, once again, has emerged as a new priority and a reminder of some enduring purposes in our work with college students which go far back into our professional legacy.

In the chapter to follow, John Whiteley and associates will examine the issue of values education from the unique perspective of how students describe the collegiate experiences which affected their value development and how they assess some of the educational interventions designed to promote values education. The authors' research provides some helpful insights into the ways in which college students perceive value development experiences and activities.

References

Astin, A. W. (1977). *Four critical years.* San Francisco: Jossey-Bass.

Barnett, D. C. & Dalton, J. C. (November, 1982). Why college students cheat. *Journal of college student personnel,* vol. 22, #6.

Bok, D. C. (1976). Can ethics be taught? *Change magazine,* #8.

Brown, R. D., & Canon, H. J. (1978). Intentional moral development as an objective of higher education. *Journal of college student personnel,* vol. 19.

Carnegie Council on Policy Studies in Higher Education. (1979). *Fair practices in higher education: Rights and responsibility of students and their colleges in a period of intensified competition for enrollment.* San Francisco: Jossey-Bass.

Chickering, A. (1969). *Education and identity.* San Francisco: Jossey-Bass.

Dalton, J. C., Barnett, D. C., & Healy, M. (1982). Educational approaches to values development in college students: A survey of NASPA chief student personnel administrators. *NASPA journal,* vol. 20, #1.

Gilligan, C. (1982). *In another voice.* Cambridge: Harvard University Press.

Hall, R. T. (1979). Moral education: A handbook for teachers. Insight and practical strategies for helping adolescents to become more caring, thoughtful, and responsible persons. *National endowment for the humanities.* Washington, D.C.

Hastings Center. (1980). *The teaching of ethics in higher education.* New York.

Kohlberg, L. (1969). Stage and sequence: The cognitive developmental approach to socialization. In D. Goslin (Ed.) *Handbook of socialization theory and research.* Chicago: Rand McNally.

Kohlberg, L. (1973). *Standard scoring manual.* Cambridge: Harvard University.

Kohlberg, L. (1979). *Assessing moral stages: A manual.* Cambridge: Center for Moral Education.

Levine, A. (1980). *When dreams and heroes died.* San Francisco: Jossey-Bass.

Lickona, T. (1976). *Moral development and behavior: Theory, research, and social issues.* New York: Holt, Rinehart, and Winston.

McBee, M. L. (Summer, 1982). Moral development: From direction to dialogue. *NASPA journal.*

Morrill, R. L. (1980). *Teaching values in college.* San Francisco: Jossey-Bass.

Muller, S. (Spring, 1982). Is your university turning out skilled barbarians? *Dialogue on campus,* Vol. XVII, #3.

Perry, W. (1970). *Forms of intellectual and ethical development in the college years.* New York: Holt, Rinehart, and Winston.

Rokeach, M. (1968). *Beliefs, attitudes, and values.* San Francisco: Jossey-Bass.

Whiteley, J. (1982). *Character development in college students,* vol. 1. Schenectady: Character Research Press.

CHAPTER THREE

Influences on Character Development During the College Years: The Retrospective View of Recent Undergraduates

by John M. Whiteley, Barbara D. Bertin, Elizabeth A. Ferrant, and Norma Yokota

The core of previous research evidence on the development of moral reasoning centers on findings that individuals differ markedly in the order and logic behind their moral judgments (Piaget, 1932; Kohlberg, 1968; Rest, 1979a), that it is possible to monitor empirically the progression of an individual's moral thinking (Colby, Gibbs, and Kohlberg, 1979; Rest, 1979a; and 1979b); and that formal education significantly affects moral judgment (Rest, 1979a; Whiteley, Bertin, and Berry, 1980; Whiteley and Associates, 1982).

A relatively recent area of inquiry on the development of moral reasoning is the identification of experiences which are associated with raising the level of moral reasoning (whether or not change in moral stage level was found to have occurred). This exploratory study reports what recent college undergraduates identified as influencing their thinking on moral issues during the college years. The instrument used for data collection was the Character Development Schedule (Ferrant, Jacobi, and Miner, 1983). It was administered to thirty-three individuals as part of the student retrospective portion of the Project Evaluation (Whiteley and Associates, 1982).

All thirty-three individuals had participated as freshmen in the Sierra Project, had resided in a residence hall which emphasized the development of a supportive community environment, and had participated in a year-long class taught within the residence hall which featured modules on community building, conflict resolution, empathy and assertion training, examination of the effects of socialization, sex and race-roles, career decision-making, and student-directed classes.

The Sierra Project was both a curricular intervention intended to foster psychological growth and raise the level of moral reasoning, and a longitudinal research study designed to measure the extent and duration of change on dimensions of character development in the transition from late adolescence to early adulthood (Whiteley and Associates, 1982). In this study, "character" was defined conceptually as understanding what is right and acting on what is right.

The Character Development Schedule (CDS) is primarily a self-report measure facilitated by an interviewer who initiates probing questions intended to clarify meanings and document more fully the opinions of the interviewee. The CDS contains forty items which explore the respondent's retrospective views on the impact which college life, people, and experiences had on them during four years of undergraduate study, as well as a specific assessment of the freshman year experience. Both open-ended and structured interview questions were utilized.

In presenting the principal results from the administration of the CDS to thirty-three recent college graduates, the format will be to organize the information provided by our respondents into *general, individual,* and *variable* themes as illustrated by relevant quotes. We have attempted to let respondents generate their own principal categories of finding and speak for themselves.

The thematic categories for reporting what respondents had to say were formulated as follows: Recurrently reported (over half of the respondents) themes identified as having significant impact were classified as *general* themes. A *variable* theme was one which had affected most students but with no consistency. A variable theme was also one over which a college or university has at least some control. Although not reported in this chapter, individual themes were also identified. These individual themes needed only to be reported by one individual.

Numerical ratings were provided by students in response to the two sections of the Character Development Schedule. First, they were asked to rate from 1 (not at all important) to 5 (very important) a series of categories of people in response to the questions, "How important were each of the following people to your character development during the college years?" Second, they were asked to rate eighteen categories of experiences on the same five point scale in response to the question, "How important were the following experiences to your character development during your college years?"

The reasons for including individually reported themes and variable themes as well as general themes are two. First, this is an exploratory study of an area of inquiry which has previously received scant attention. Second, the Sierra Project sample is not a random student population on the campus of the University of California, Irvine, and generalization from these results are limited. It was believed, therefore, that future researchers examining experiences which impact character development during the college years would benefit from a fuller anecdotal record of what was reported by our respondents. Construction of new scales or other approaches to data collection would be facilitated.

General Theme: The Importance of Community

The general theme of the importance and effects of community was a pervasive one in our sample, reflecting the emphasis which had been placed by the staff in designing and implementing the Sierra Project. Students chose to comment about three facets of community: the positive sense of closeness, camaraderie, and family; the effects of the supportive living-learning environment; and the quality of interactions with professional and student staff and faculty.

As can be seen from the following quote, many of our interviewees report the presence of a high level of community within Sierra and, more importantly, positively assess the impact of this sense of community on their college experiences.

> I remember the warmth, the communication, the sense of community. Everybody basically had the same goals. We were in Sierra for a particular reason . . . one was to try to eliminate some of the negative aspects that exist around UCI, such as the isolation, the alienation, so that everybody won't be so cold to each other.

Sierra provided a context in which students lived and learned together in an environment which fostered feelings of security, support, and personal belonging. This aspect of the educational intervention was based on the premise that fostering a psychological sense of community can positively affect individual growth and interaction.

A second quote reflects the interviewees' assessment of Sierra's educational approach and their views on how the environment and curriculum contributed to learning and sharing.

> The freedom that Sierra provided . . . they tried the best they could to present us with a learning environment, to be open to a lot of things, like aspects of sexuality, religion, and interpersonal relations. Just to be open and see what suits your needs. They didn't really push anything to do; they offered things for you to take.

Within the Sierra program, residents worked closely with student and professional staff. Student staff served as peer advisers and counselors, teaching assistants, participant-observers, role models and friends. The professional staff functioned as teachers and psychologists, offering instructional experience designed to foster new skills and understanding. This third quote deals specifically with the student and professional staff involved in the Sierra Project and gives us a picture of the numerous ways in which they influenced and were seen by students.

> They had been through a year or two, and they knew what it was like, what we were going through . . . they were able to keep above us, by helping us and putting on classes, but they were also able to relate to us as friends.

The foregoing self-reports suggest that the importance of community was quite pervasive, especially the psychological sense of community, the supportive living-learning environment, and the quality of interactions with professional and student staff and faculty.

Commentary on the General Theme of Community

The impact of institutions and influence of academic programs on undergraduate students have been areas of increasing concern to educators in recent years. Sandeen (1976) has argued that the "sense of being a student" is not as prevalent on college campuses today as in the past. He recognizes that student involvement can play an effective role in the development of a sense of community. Because the transition to college is a time of rapid role and environmental change, as well as a period of potential developmental change, it can present difficulties as well as opportunities for students.

One frequent negative consequence arising from rapid change is a reduction in one's sense of community. Knox (1977) has indicated that a lack of community can undermine one's sense of security in the face of changing circumstances and result in an inability to make decisions. He states: "When confronted with a welter of conflicting choices and no clear sense of direction, the safest course of actions seems to be no action at all. When there are so many pressures to respond, people may fail to notice that they are no longer initiating but only reacting" (p. 47).

General Theme: Exposure to Diversity

Commentary on the effects of exposure to diversity was recurrent in the structured interviews. It is our belief that exposure to diversity was singled out for a combination of three reasons. First, the residents of Sierra were diverse: it was a coed hall consisting of an even number of men and women; it was multicultural, with a roughly even distribution from year to year of Anglos, Blacks, Chicanos, and Asian Americans; and there was a wide range in socio- economic backgrounds and level of academic potential (previous performance and SAT-scores). Second, explicit attention was given to heightening the impact of diversity through the curricular experiences in the form of conflict resolution (and conflict inducement), empathy training, and modules on socialization, sex-roles, and race-roles. Third, the residents of Sierra were predominantly Stage 3 in their level of moral reasoning. This means that their primary referent for reasoning about moral issues were the opinions of those around them. As entering freshmen, loss of their previous primary referent groups (family members, high school friends and peers) created a void. The context of a close psychological community in Sierra Hall provided a new primary referent group. Exposure to student diversity, therefore, had a greater impact than it would have in the context of a continuing close relationship to old support groups.

Two general types of influence are reflected in the following quotes: namely, living with and getting to know people from other ethnic, socioeconomic and religious backgrounds and the resulting exposure to different values and beliefs; and classes in Sierra which facilitated discussions of these different values and beliefs. These responses highlight the various ways in which exposure to a diversity of viewpoints can benefit students.

It led to being open minded and listening to other's opinions and respecting them. I asked myself why I believed in the things I do.

Discussions with certain people helped me explore my own feelings and convictions. Putting it into words in a way that I can explain it to them and to myself. By hearing different viewpoints and pointing out ambiguities in their theories and in mine, I think it helped to re-evaluate where I was at . . . I think it leads to change sometimes and other times it strengthens.

Commentary on the General Theme of Diversity

Students chose to report experiences with diversity as quite influential. While one source of the impact was undoubtedly the structured interactions in a coed multicultural group among a predominantly conventional (Stage 3) population, the interactions also occurred during a time in their lives when young people attempt to formulate personalized belief systems. During this stage of their development, discussions with peers play an important role in modifying the values students bring to college. Many young people lack familiarity with different cultures and the value orientations of people from different socio-economic groups. They often hold stereotypic beliefs about persons from different ethnic groups as well. Exposure to a diversity of cultural and value orientations can result in a broadened worldview, a breaking down of stereotypes, and a greater tolerance and acceptance of differing values and beliefs.

General Theme: The Significance of Interpersonal Relationships

The significance of interpersonal relationships to the development of adolescents and in the transition from late adolescence to early adulthood is well established. It is not surprising, therefore, that recent college undergraduates reported that interpersonal relationships had been influential to their development during the college years. The structured interview format of the Character Development Survey, however, made it possible to identify the specific relevance of interpersonal relationships to the development of character. The first insights centered on the impact which friendships had on these conventional students. Friends were a source of approval and support in times of difficulty. The following quotes are representative:

> Friends are important to me. What they think is important . . . a lot of things you do for their feedback or their approval.

> They are important when they are there when you
> need them. There are so many trials and tribulations
> you go through and if you have someone there to help
> you out, it helps you get through these hard times.

The Sierra Project curriculum fostered relationships within the community. The effect of this emphasis on students is also reflected in the roles which friends played:

> We were like a family in a way, were so tight it was like
> a close knit family.

> It was a lot of help, to just talk it out and it was some-
> thing very supportive; we supported each other in our
> talks.

Nurtured over the course of an academic year, and formed at a time of transition from high school to college, some friendships developed during the Freshman year had an enduring quality:

> We stayed friends for four years and still are friends
> . . . you really trust what they value and where each of
> us has been successful, to try to emulate each other.

Despite careful probing, it did not appear that peer friendships had a specific impact on character development.

Respondents to the Character Development Survey singled out intimate heterosexual relationships as influencing their character development. In the general interview format of the CDS, however, it was not possible to determine with any degree of specificity what it had been about intimate relationships that influenced character:

> I think (these experiences regarding intimate part-
> ners) made me more mature.

> It was a whole different learning experience . . . he was
> different from me . . . he came from a different back-
> ground.

Rather than offering specifics, our respondents chose to refer to generalities like increasing maturity, motivation, and support.

The experiences involved in ending intimate relationships were presented by our respondents as influential on their character, although the connections were not apparent from what they said.

> It made me stronger . . . I had been dependent on him for much of my happiness and my day to day dealings . . . (in regards to breaking up with boyfriend).

> It's like learning, I'd do it all differently if I had to do it all over again . . . (in regard to an intimate relationship).

It is important to recognize that while respondents did not make the connection with character issues such as the moral and ethical challenges in intimate relationships, they did report on the significance of them. Future researchers need to develop instruments which allow the discovery of the connections which exist according to the retrospective reports of college students.

A third area of interpersonal relationships which former college students reported as influencing their character were those with family:

> I wanted to break the bond of dependency that I had with them . . . and I'm constantly fighting with them to let go . . . let me think and do as I will.

> They have always influenced me as far as my future goals, what I should strive for and all that.

The themes with family centered on independence and dependence, and reflect the autonomy concerns covered in the next section. Again, the connections with character were not drawn.

A fourth area of interpersonal relationships reported by roughly half of the sample were those with staff and faculty. Because of their uneven and inconsistent quality, they are discussed in a separate section on variable themes.

General Theme: Autonomy

In contrast to the general theme on interpersonal relationships, where it was difficult to determine from our respondents what it was about the relationships that influenced their character development, the responses on the autonomy theme were noteworthy for their explicitness.

In addition to the explicitness, the autonomy theme was noteworthy for the number of facets (sub-themes) which students said influenced their character. Five facets of autonomy were distinguished: the immediate consequence of physical separation from family, the changed nature of relationships between parents and children, the continuing role which parents do play in the newfound autonomy, the opportunities for decision making and the consequences of those decisions, and taking responsibility for oneself or others.

The first facet, the immediate consequences of physical separation from family, appeared to be characterized by not feeling dependent (and feeling more independent), by exercising more responsibility and by greater personal openness:

> I was no longer under the influence of my parents . . . I had so much more freedom to say and do things that I would not have done had I been at home . . . I was more free to experiment.

The college environment provides a marked contrast to the family setting:

> It gave me the chance to really experience life as it really is on my own without my family . . . my ten brothers and sisters . . . it made a big difference going from a family to being by myself . . . it helped me to concentrate on me . . . not on everybody else.

The second facet, the changed nature of relationships between parents and children, was approached by respondents from a number of different perspectives. One perspective was the increasing "adult to adult" nature of the interactions, and the increased appreciation of what parents do contribute that is positive:

> During the end of high school and the beginning of college you say, "I have the dumbest parents in the world—they don't know anything." And then when you graduate you realize just how stupid you really were and how much more they know than you—if just because they lived longer than you—and you really come to value them.

Another perspective was the lessening influence of parents, a perspective sometimes couched in terms implying rebellion:

> When you're at home you're so much influenced by your parents that anything that is outside of what they teach you is taboo—not that extreme but it is something that is out of bounds for you.

> You open yourself to more of what you want your character to be like . . . you're not under your parents anymore so you're making up your own character, you're picking from here and there, . . . it's a gradual maturation process.

Parents do play a continuing role in the newfound autonomy which students reported was so attractive to them, and this continuing role varied greatly across our population:

> My dependency was not only financial but also emotional. It was very bad. I saw going away to school and living in the dorm the first step of breaking that bond even though I knew I had to do it personally and on an emotional level.

> I knew they were there when I needed them . . . they helped me develop my character by listening, by offering suggestions, by sharing their wisdom and experiences.

The respondents singled out the opportunities for decision-making and the consequences of those decisions as impactful on their characters, though the linkages were not implicit:

> It forced me to make decisions—to look to your self for decisions—and to take responsibility for yourself . . . I learned a lot about myself, my limitations and also about how much more I had to give.

> I had to define what I really wanted, such as what would make me happy . . . I still haven't found that— that's one of the problems. I'm still searching for what I really want to do. You know, what's really going to make it for me. In that sense, I do have a lot of growing to do.

In the area of decision-making, such topics as not having to justify oneself, setting up personal priorities, taking responsibility, and the opportunity to decide for oneself were intertwined with strong identity concerns.

Taking responsibility for oneself, and sometimes others, was a fifth facet of autonomy. It was reported in the context of our investigation of the factors which influenced the development of character, we believe, because of its importance to students as a growth accomplishment for them:

> Character is finding a balance between selfishness and selflessness. And when you have to come first and when others have to come first, that's what's always changing . . . and when you are put in a position of having responsibility for someone else, that forces the issue. It's a learning experience of when who comes first.

> I had to be able to tell myself what I could and couldn't do . . . it made me more aware of the type of person I was—both my strengths and limitations, what I was capable of doing and what I was limited in.

The notion of being able to decide when to do something for oneself and when to do it for others was extraordinarily attractive.

Commentary on the General Theme of Autonomy

Autonomy was clearly an important theme to our respondents, and they felt it had been very influential in both their growth in character and their growth in general. As a psychological concept relevant to understanding the transition from late adolescence to early adulthood, autonomy has been of significance in the theoretical and research literature. Autonomy, for example, is one of Chickering's (1969) seven vectors of student development. Based on the retrospective commentary by recent undergraduates, it appears that the experiences involved in the attainment of autonomy are influential in the development of character.

Variable Theme: The Importance of Interactions with Faculty and Staff

The importance of interactions with faculty and staff to the development of character has been separated out as a variable theme because of the extraordinary diversity of response, and because it is a theme on which an institution of higher education has exceptional control.

The respondents to our interview report that an important aspect of their learning experiences and development in college was the role model/mentor relationships they had with faculty, TA's and other campus professionals. As might well be expected, a few respondents also note the lack of or negative faculty relationships they experienced. Together, these quotes give us some insight into the types of influence campus professionals exert on undergraduates.

> They (professors and TA's) were influential in helping me to develop my character and decide what was right and wrong for me. I saw that they were older and yet they had kind of modern ideas. It kind of strengthened some of my more modern or liberal ideas.

> In discussion, he (TA) got us to discuss how we felt . . . that made me more aware of myself and other people. It matured me and opened my eyes more to looking more into life.

> They (campus professionals) could be very understanding to the types of things you were experiencing . . . Some offered guidance, some were able to provide a parental type of role. They helped me to develop my ability to think, to reason and to be logical about things—to think for myself, then to develop my own ideals and character.

Commentary on Variable Theme

The preceding remarks *highlight* the range of influence that interactions with campus professionals exert on college students. In his study of the impact of college on student's personal, social and vocational development, Astin (1977) found that student-faculty interaction had a positive effect on student satisfaction regarding all aspects of their college experience. In fact, frequency of student-faculty interaction showed a stronger positive relationship to student satisfaction than to any other research variable, including courses, friendships, and the intellectual environment. After an extensive review of the literature on college impact, Sandeen (1976) also argued that the impact of the faculty upon students was one of the most important aspects of the educational process. He summarized his assessment as follows: "Students desire and need an effective learning relationship with faculty, so that they can mature intellectually under the guidance of an expert who knows them and cares about them" (p. 82).

Influence of Selected People and Experiences on Character Development

This section reports student responses to two general questions asking them to assess the importance of persons and experiences to their character development during the college years on a five point scale ranging from 1 (not at all important) to 5 (very important).

The first question asked "How important were each of the following people to your character development during the college Years?" Respondents were given seven categories of persons to rate plus an "other" category. The results were as follows:

Table 1

How important were each of the following people to your character development during the college years? (1 = not at all; 5 = very important)

	n	Mean	Standard
Close friends/peers	33	4.03	1.04
Sierra Staff	33	3.64	1.03
An intimate partner	31	3.48	1.18
Parents	33	3.48	1.50
Professors/TAs	33	3.12	1.05
Other relatives	33	2.09	1.04
Priest/Minister/Rabbi	25	2.08	1.12
Other people	6*	4.17*	0.75

*When the raw data were examined, it turned out that one individual reported legitimately an "other" person: namely an individual met in outside employment. The other five fit into existing categories (other relatives, the principal classroom instructor in Sierra; Sierra student staff).

Least influential were "other relative" and "priests, ministers, rabbis." The third least influential category was "professors/TA," a group which has been discussed above under "variable themes."

Of the categories of choice specified by the Character Development Schedule, the most influential were "close friends/peers" and "Sierra staff." The third most influential category was a tie between "parents" and "an intimate partner."

The second question asked, "How important were each of the following experiences to your character development during your college years?" The Results were as follows:

Table 2

How important were the following experiences to your character development during your college years?

	n*	Mean	Standard Deviation
Living away from home	33	4.58	0.71
Assuming additional responsibility for self	33	4.36	0.70
Discussing values and morals	33	4.30	0.73
Getting to know different people**	33	3.94	1.09
Extra curricular activities	31	3.74	1.03
Assuming responsibility for another	30	3.40	1.07
Reading books	32	3.38	0.94
Classes	33	3.37	0.08
Internship/research activities	24	3.21	1.25
Travel	29	3.20	1.32
Human Potential & Self help movement	26	3.12	1.21
Experiencing tragedy or suffering	26	3.12	1.37
Religious or spiritual experience	30	3.10	1.16
Community service activities	31	2.90	1.16
Psychological counseling	15	2.80	1.15
Any other experiences not listed	3	2.67	1.15
Involvement in political activities	21	2.19	1.17
Watching movies or T.V.	33	1.97	1.01

*Number of respondents varies due to the option of a "not applicable" response
**People from cultures, races or socio-economic groups other than your own

Least influential were: "watching movies or television," "involvement in political activities," "psychological counseling," and "community service activities." The most influential experiences were: "living away from home," "assuming additional responsibility for yourself," "discussing values and morals," and "getting to know different people on campus."

The final items from the Character Development Schedule are of interest. They asked respondents to indicate on a five point scale (1 = least; 5 = most) how important they considered the college years to be to their character development, and how much they thought they changed during those years. The results were as follows:

Table 3

	n	Mean	Standard Deviation
How important were the years you spent in college to your character development?	32	4.59	.56
How much do you think your character changed during college years?	33	4.12	.70

It is apparent that our respondents considered the college years to have been very significant to their character development. Parenthetically, many of the respondents objected to the wording of the above question regarding how much they had changed during the college years. They had difficulty with the idea of having changed, and consistently reported that they had not really "changed" but rather had "developed" over the course of their college education. A revision of the CDS now in preparation will reword this question accordingly.

Conclusion

This is a report of an exploratory investigation of the influences on character development during the college years based on the retrospective assessments of recent college undergraduates. The limitations of this report are several:

1. The sample was influenced by having been participants in the Sierra Project during their freshman year, and, as such, they were not representative of the student population as a whole of the institution from which they graduated.

2. Small size of sample.

3. The data source is limited by its retrospective character. While retrospective commentary is a valuable data source, multiple sources of data would have enriched the analysis.

4. The generalizations from this analysis are limited by the fact that the sample was restricted to but one of a number of diverse institutions of higher education in this country.

Nonetheless, the retrospective commentaries by recent undergraduates did reveal that four general themes (the importance of community, exposure to diversity, the significance of interpersonal relationships, and autonomy) and one variable theme (the importance of interactions with faculty and staff) were viewed by respondents as positively impacting their character development. The explicit linkages of important psychological experiences to the development of character were not provided in some instances. Nonetheless, it is now possible to undertake additional investigations of which experiences potentially have an impact on the development of character in college students.

References

Astin, A. W. (1977). *Four critical years.* San Francisco: Jossey-Bass.

Chickering, A. W. (1969). *Education and identity.* San Francisco: Jossey-Bass.

Colby, A., Gibbs, J., & Kohlberg, L. (1979). *The assessment of moral judgment standard form scoring manual.* Cambridge, MA: Moral Education Research Foundation.

Ferrant, E. A., Jacobi, M. A., & Miner, J. K. (1983). *Character development schedule.* Unpublished interview schedule, University of California, Irvine.

Knox, A. B. (1977). *Adult development and learning.* San Francisco: Jossey-Bass.

Kohlberg, L. (1958). The development of modes of moral thinking and choice in the years ten to sixteen. Unpublished doctoral dissertation, University of Chicago.

Piaget, J. (1965). *The moral judgment of the child.* New York: Free Press. (Originally published, 1932.)

Rest, J. R. (1979a). *Development in judging moral issues.* Minneapolis: University of Minnesota Press.

Rest, J. R. (1979b). The impact of higher education on moral judgment development. (Technical Report No. 5). Minnesota Moral Research Projects.

Sandeen, A. (1976). *Undergraduate education: conflict in change.* Lexington, MA: Lexington Books, D.C. Heath & Co.

Whiteley, J. M. & Associates. (1982). *Character development in college students.* New York: Character Research Press.

Whiteley, J. M., Bertin, B. C. & Berry, B. A. (1980). Research on the development of moral reasoning of college students. In M. L. McBee (Ed.) *Rethinking college responsibilities for values.* San Francisco: Jossey-Bass.

CHAPTER FOUR

Critical Factors in the Value Development Process

by Jon C. Dalton

Within the last two decades considerable research has been conducted on the process by which individuals develop moral values and how they learn to think ethically. Lawrence Kohlberg's work on moral development theory provided an important conceptual framework for examining the development of moral reasoning. Much of the research based on the theory and field studies of Kohlberg have focused on young children. More recently, however, studies have been specifically designed to assess moral development in college students. The Sierra Project at the University of California, Irvine (see Whiteley, 1982), Boyd's (1979) moral education study at St. Louis University, Rest's (1979) moral judgment research at the University of Minnesota, Sprinthall's (1978) research on moral reasoning in late adolescents, and Mentkowski's (1980) work with the Alverno Program at Alverno College are some examples of efforts to explore ways in which students' ability to think about issues of right and wrong can be enhanced.

As Sandeen indicates in Chapter One, value development has always been an important concern in college student personnel work. The research and writings of student development researchers such as E. G. Williamson, Esther Lloyd-Jones, Nevitt Sanford, Clyde Parker, Arthur Chickering, and Theodore Miller all recognized the importance of the ethical dimension of personality growth and development in college students. Only since Kohlberg, however, has moral development been studied in such depth as a unique dimension of college student development. One of the benefits of such specialized research is that we know considerably more than ever before about the primary factors which encourage the development of moral thinking and awareness in late adolescents. In the remainder of this chapter these factors will be summarized and discussed in terms of their relevance for college student personnel work. Although there is disagreement about how these factors interrelate, most researchers agree that each of these factors is important in understanding how and why moral development occurs.

1. Social Perspective-Taking

One of the fundamental conditions for moral value development is the ability to consider things from another's perspective. Unless a college student is able to empathize with other people and gain an appreciation of their specific thoughts, feelings and ways of viewing the world, they will be isolated in their own subjectivity. The development of social perspective-taking requires the ability to recognize that there are a variety of perspectives on moral issues, and that others share many similarities both in the moral issues they encounter and the manner in which they attempt to deal with them. Being able to take the perspective of others is a necessary pre-condition for moral development (see Meyer, 1976).

Some argue (see Kohlberg, 1975) that there is a universal human tendency toward empathy or role-taking which naturally leads to concern about justice, reciprocity, and equality. There is, however, considerable variation in the development of social perspective-taking and evidence that some individuals never achieve a "moral" perspective.

The important role of social perspective-taking in character development has been confirmed in the research of Selman (1976) and Mosher and Sprinthall (1975). Their findings indicate a relationship between increased ability to empathize and increased level of moral reasoning. Empathy allows a person to "feel" another's needs and feelings while social perspective-taking enables one to perceive how another person might think about issues and why they think the way they do. This ability to "feel" for another and to perceive their point of view is crucial in stimulating more complex and sophisticated ways of thinking.

Social perspective-taking is especially important in the college setting because of the availability of so many points of view on issues and problems. The college environment represents an ideal setting in which one's own perspective can be enhanced through interactions with others whose viewpoints are different. These interactions promote role-taking and encourage a more reflective approach toward moral conflict issues.

The decline in student altruism over the decades of the 1970s (see Astin, 1977, 1984) suggests that college students may be less inclined to care about others' perspectives and feelings. Levine (1980) documents the narcissism or privatism which seems to characterize recent college students. Because of uncertainty about the future, increasing competition for jobs, and more materialistic values, college students appear to be less flexible and interested in things outside their immediate sphere of interest.

Social perspective-taking is especially important in the college setting because for most students it may be their first experience in confronting such a multiplicity of viewpoints, lifestyles, and values. Rokeach (1975) claims that self-awareness is the opposite side of social awareness and is promoted through the development of social perspective-taking. As students are able to appreciate others' points of view they are more likely to develop respect for the rights and needs of others. Lickona (1976) argues that recognition of others' rights and needs leads naturally to concern about issues of fairness and responsibility. Carol Gilligan's (1982) important research on the perspectives unique in women's moral development reveals a special concern for caring for others and taking responsibility for their welfare.

Some educators (see Hersh, 1980) feel that one of the most effective methods of promoting social perspective-taking is through experiences of caring for another person. By having to be responsible for another's welfare in a caring relationship, one often gains considerable insight into the other's circumstances and point of view. This experience can help to generate empathy and a personal identification with the experiences of others. Involvement in college activities such as peer advising, residence halls staff, tutoring, volunteer activities, or just helping out a friend in trouble, are examples of ways in which caring for another can promote greater social perspective-taking.

2. Stage Development in Moral Reasoning

One of the most important contributions of recent research on moral development is the recognition that moral development occurs through a series of cumulative and hierarchical stages. Each stage is characterized by an underlying organization of thought which gives it unity and coherence. Moreover, each stage of moral reasoning builds upon each preceding stage in an orderly progression of increasing complexity and sophistication. These features make it possible to examine the form of moral reasoning by means of characteristic stage features. Since these features are universal and invariant it is also possible to assess individuals' moral stage level and to intervene in ways to promote development to higher stages.

Lawrence Kohlberg identified six stages of moral thinking from his interviews with research subjects. Kohlberg demonstrated that the differences in how people reason about important ethical decisions could best be explained by a theory of moral development in which individuals progressed through a series of moral reasoning stages. Moreover, considerable research has confirmed Kohlberg's finding that moral development can be promoted by exposing individuals to moral dilemma problems and to stage thinking one level above their own. This discovery has provided a highly useful educational strategy which has already been employed by a number of student personnel practitioners in such areas as residence halls assignments, leadership training, counseling groups, and classroom discussions.

Because moral development progresses through identifiable stages, efforts to promote values education must start with students where they are developmentally. The student development professional must be able to assess individual moral development and to devise educational interventions that are targeted to specific stage levels. Frequent use has been made of hypothetical moral dilemmas as one practical means for educational intervention. By involving students in discussing moral dilemma situations, they can be exposed to higher stages of moral reasoning and encouraged to assimilate more complex moral thinking into their own cognitive outlook.

Carol Gilligan (1982) has challenged Kohlberg's account of moral development by arguing that his theory is based upon male experiences and perspectives and, consequently, has a built-in bias. Her research on female subjects presents an alternate view of moral development which stresses the importance of caring, empathy and social responsibility.

It is important to note that moral reasoning development occurs slowly, generally in fractions of stages over long periods of time. Consequently, moral development interventions should be conducted and evaluated throughout the collegiate years for maximum impact.

3. Community

Students' experience of a strong sense of community in the educational setting can contribute substantially to their development of values. Heath (1968) found that one of the important factors for maturing was the communal character of the college. He found that the sense of "community" in an institution is heightened when there is internal coherence of purposes and where values and goals are consistently integrated into college activities and role-modeling by staff and faculty.

The experience of community provides students with a support system which makes it easier for them to experiment and take risks more freely. This important interaction between the individual and community on matters of values is more likely to occur where there is strong perception of community on campus. Arthur Levine (1980) points out that one important measure of community is how strongly students believe they can profit from cooperation from the community. If they do not identify with the values of the community, students will not be inclined to regard them as significant in their own lives.

Students' perceptions of community is influenced to a great extent by how students are treated in the community. Hersh

(1980) reports that when he surveyed 800 students about critical events that occurred to them in the educational community they identified consideration for one's needs, feelings, and interests as an important positive factor.

4. Peer Culture

There seems little doubt from the research that the values prized in the peer culture are highly influential for value development in college students. Students derive values from those they admire. Unfortunately, there are many values that have been acquired by the peer culture without much critical examination. The problem for student personnel staff is that they find the peer culture difficult to influence or change. In larger institutions it is especially difficult to influence the peer culture because, to a large extent, it operates outside the academic community.

One of the reasons that the peer group influence is so strong is that college students are, in general, most likely to develop close relationships with those who share common interests in a common environment. As T. M. Newcomb argues, "Many of the problems of the late adolescent in our society are the kind that invite college students to share them with each other" (see Newcomb, 1979, p. 141). Moreover, Kohlberg's research indicates most college students are in stage III (conventional morality) and very dependent upon each others' opinions. Most new college students face problems of establishing independence and new interpersonal relationships while mastering a complicated and threatening new environment at the very time in life when they are in search of identity. These common problems draw students together and help to create strong peer groups which have considerable influence on students' attitudes and values.

In a small college the entire student body may constitute a homogeneous peer group because of its size. In larger institutions many peer groups may develop around common social and educational interests. As college populations increase in diversity, peer groups increase in numbers and variety on campus. This fact alone makes it more difficult for student affairs staff to stay abreast of peer culture and to be able to influence it in a way that promotes positive value development in students.

Because peer groups exercise such significant influence on values development in college students, student affairs staff should include the peer culture in their on-going student life research. Even though the peer culture may be difficult to change, it is important to understand its values and how it affects college students.

It is interesting to note that some religious groups on campus have made significant use of peer group influence as a strategy for recruiting and proselytizing new members. One common approach is to have initial student contacts made by peers and to include new members in small groups which provide powerful peer group support and influence. This strategy has proven to be highly effective although not without criticism by those who feel that such peer group tactics can be excessively coercive especially for new students entering the college environment.

Student affairs staff have also recognized the effectiveness of using student peers in many areas of service and programming. For example, student peers are very effective in disseminating information. In intramural sports and student activities we have learned how to use peer group loyalty, identity, and esprit de corps to promote recreational and educational programs. Peers are used in counseling, residence halls staffing, academic advising, tutoring, orientation, and in many other areas of service delivery. One of the advantages of such peer involvement is that student peers have almost instant credibility with students and help to give credibility to the values which may be conveyed on behalf of student affairs staff. Student peers, for example, can talk to other students about responsible alcohol use with a rapport and credibility which would be very difficult for most student affairs staff to achieve.

Because it is so influential on value development in college students, it is important that student affairs staff understand the peer culture on their campus and develop techniques designed to enable the peer culture to contribute as much as possible to important values education objectives of the institution.

5. Role Models

One of the most powerful influences upon student development is *moral example*. Douglas Heath (1968) found in this research at Haverford College that students' integration of values
was encouraged by their relation to staff who served as moral
examples. William Perry (1970) reached much the same conclusion in his research at Harvard. He found that value commitments in college students were directly influenced by educators
who themselves had an open style in which their values,
doubts, and personal commitments were visible to students.
The power of moral example is that it conveys values directly
through personal commitment and action. Role modeling is particularly influential for many students who are exploring value
commitments and lifestyles. Moreover, students are generally
so accustomed to having values laid out directly in the home, in
their church or synagogue and school that they resist such efforts by the time they get to college. Role modeling, on the other
hand, puts values in action and teaches through example.

Student affairs staff can be powerful role models. They tend
to embody the institutions for many students since they are the
ones who explain procedures, serve as advocates, and provide
advice and personal assistance. Student polls often show that
students know their student affairs staff and have closer ties to
them more than anyone other than peers. This makes the role
modeling potential of student affairs staff very significant for
students.

With the demise of *in loco parentis*, many student affairs
staff adopted a value-neutral style in which they felt they must
avoid all appearances of value commitment. In an effort to be
"neutral" so as to avoid "meddling and moralizing," they took a
laissez faire approach toward moral issues which, for all practical purposes, resulted in non-involvement in value issues. Unfortunately, this value neutral approach was often interpreted
by students as a lack of concern about values. Smith and Peterson (1977) claim that the non-directive style vis-a-vis students
conveys a tolerating, non-judgmental attitude but also the impression that values are entirely relative to individuals and situations. In the final analysis value neutrality proves ineffective

because it simply doesn't work. In practice the "hidden agenda" of values always comes through and students are quick to pick up the implicit hypocrisy of such double messages (Rokeach, 1975, p.124)

Role modeling provides one of the more effective ways to avoid "preaching" at students while at the same time affirming values in a manner which can have a powerful impact upon students. While it is important to avoid any appearance of indoctrination of values in the performance of one's professional duties, this does not mean that student affairs staff must suppress their personal value convictions in their interactions with students and colleagues. It is one thing to tell students what to believe and prize, it is quite another to *demonstrate* values in the context of one's personal conduct.

In the author's (Dalton, et al., 1982) survey of NASPA chief student personnel administrators reported in chapter two, almost 2/3 of the respondents reported that role modeling was the most effective activity for transmitting values to students. Eighty-five percent of the respondents reported that they actively promoted role modeling by their staff and sixty-six percent indicated that role modeling was their *primary* means of promoting values among students. These findings indicate that student affairs staff recognize the important influence role models can have on moral development in college students and actively seek to promote it.

William Bennett concludes that "There is no way to do anything about the formation of character in the young unless you have at hand people . . . who make some effort to live the difference, and who have an interest in instilling that difference in others" (Bennett, 1980, p. 27).

6. Interaction with Persons of Differing Values and Viewpoints

Douglas Heath (1968) reports that an important factor in promoting values awareness and development in students is the experience of being confronted and challenged by others' values and lifestyles. Such experiences tend to encourage and even demand reflectiveness and re-examination of what one may know or believe. Students who are isolated or resist encounters with others who hold contrasting values are likely to be rigidly tied to an unexamined set of values. Moreover, when values are unexamined they may be superficial as well as self-serving.

Resnikoff and Jennings (1980) found in their study of a sample of students in the Sierra Project that experiences with others which presented a discrepancy of values and beliefs tended to promote changes in moral development reasoning. Learning how to disagree with another's values and beliefs without rejecting them as persons was an important means of clarifying and testing one's own values. Their research confirmed what Heath had found, that development is promoted as one engages with others in clarifying and defending one's own values.

Colleges and universities generally provide ideal settings for students to interact with persons of differing values and lifestyles. The mix of nationalities, ages, rural and urban backgrounds, racial and religious differences that are present on most campuses provide many practical opportunities for students to compare and contrast their own values with those around them.

In his examination of social role taking stages, Meyer (1980) concluded that interacting with others whose values are different helps one to move beyond the lowest stages of self interest and egocentrism to the higher levels of mutual and social role taking. This interaction with others, particularly those who are different than oneself, appears to be a significant factor in the development of a more complex and integrated set of personal values.

7. Experiences Which Challenge One's Way of Thinking

The encounter and struggle with experiences which challenge one's own beliefs and values can be very influential in promoting value development in college students. Such experiences challenge one's way of thinking and often force a re-examination of values. The values which are judged to be inadequate or inconsistent tend to be discarded and new value commitments are confirmed.

College provides many occasions in which students encounter such challenging experiences. New students come to college generally in a state of heightened vulnerability. They are often anxious about making friends and succeeding academically. At the same time they are usually establishing a more independent life style by moving away from parents into a new living environment. This environment often imposes new patterns of daily living and a variety of new relationships and social interactions. These changes in the individual's environment often force new adaptions and adjustments in one's values and moral reasoning. These environmental forces converge in the college setting to challenge and disrupt students' way of thinking and valuing. It is this set of circumstances which makes the college environment so potentially influential for promoting values development in students.

Some developmental theorists such as Erikson, Heath, and Chickering believe that these situations of challenge are so important to individual development that they should be intentionally promoted. Heath (1968) argued that "disorganizing" experiences for students are very important in the educational process. Educators must intentionally challenge the values of students in order to promote more mature and consistent values. Heath feels that the freshman year is an especially good time to help students confront value issues since they are "particularly receptive to the exploration of their inner life and that of others" (see Heath, 1968, p. 260). Erikson (1968) describes the pivotal role of stage "crisis" in individual development and the importance of encouraging and supporting the individual's successful resolution of these life "turning points." This is particularly true at the late adolescent stages where identity formation is the central "crisis."

Chickering (1969), in summarizing his analysis of how development occurs in students, concludes that development occurs through sequences of differentiation and integration. It is, he argues, one of the most important principles of learning but one that is very often ignored. "Differentiation" requires a challenge or disruption of one's way of thinking. Students' moral thinking must be sufficiently challenged in order to develop responses which help them to integrate conflicting values.

When students encounter such challenging experiences, it is important that they have a support system available. The dilemma for student personnel staff is knowing how to achieve a proper balance between introducing disequilibrium while, at the same time, maintaining support. Obviously, many experiences which offer a strong potential for development also contain a significant potential for damage. As Sanford describes it, the role of the educator is to "find challenges that are sufficient to require that the individual make a really new kind of adaption, but not so intense or disturbing as to force the student to fall back on earlier primitive modes of adaption which will serve him badly in the long run" (see Sanford, 1979, p. 13). We will discuss in the next chapter some practical strategies for the delicate task of promoting conflict and resolution in values development.

8. Decision-Making

Decision-making, both in real and hypothetical situations, has been found to stimulate moral awareness and development. Mattox (1975) claims that discussions and decision-making about moral issues are needed for moral growth. Deciding between conflicting alternatives forces students to evaluate their own morality. Likewise, Kohlberg (1975) found that the process of examination and evaluation of moral thinking was promoted by hypothetical dilemmas in which individuals were asked to choose among alternative actions. Allen (1975) argues that value development is encouraged through the exercise of moral reasoning, especially by examining one's own decisions in real and hypothetical situations. Morrill (1980) believes that an awareness of personal values can be heightened by the process of comparison and contrast which is stimulated through decision-making situations.

There is general agreement in the research on moral development that the disequilibrium produced through decisions involving moral conflicts helps to promote moral development. Such situations force individuals to reexamine values and beliefs and to test their adequacy in the face of challenging moral situations. Dissonance is produced whenever personal values and beliefs are experienced as inadequate for resolving new moral conflicts. This dissonance naturally encourages a process of development in which more adequate forms of reasoning and decision-making are promoted. This disturbance is often perceived as a threat or risk by students and care should always be taken to provide support in such situations (see Morrill, 1980, p. 87). Nevitt Sanford provides a thoughtful critique of the educational potential of intellectual disequilibrium:

> We could run an institution in the interest of positive mental health that would so protect individuals from challenging stimuli that they would not develop at all. They might remain quite healthy but very simple, underdeveloped people. They don't have problems because they are so insensitive that they are not aware of the things that would arouse problems in other people. Similarly, you can have a highly developed person who is complex, tortured, and full of conflicts but a rich and interesting person (see Sanford, 1979, p. 283).

College life presents students with many choices about values in which a variety of decisions must be made. The abundance of these decision-making opportunities during the college years make higher education a very powerful environment for promoting moral development in students.

Summary

The eight topics discussed in this chapter represent important factors in the value development process for college students. Together, they help to provide an agenda for student development interventions designed to promote values development. In Chapter Five, and effort will be made to design a comprehensive program model for values development which incorporates these nine important factors.

References

Allen, R. F. (1975). But the earth abideth forever: Values in environmental education. In John Meyer, et al. *Values education*. Waterloo, Ontario: Wilfrid Laurier Press.

Astin, A. (1977). *Four critical years: Effects of college on beliefs, attitudes, and knowledge*. San Francisco: Jossey-Bass.

Astin, A. (1984). *ACE-CIRP profile of entering students*. Los Angeles: UCLA.

Bennett, W. J. (1980). The teacher, the curriculum, and values education development. In Mary McBee (Ed.) *Rethinking college responsibilities for values*. New Directions for Higher Education, #31. San Francisco: Jossey-Bass.

Boyd, D. (1976). Education toward principled moral judgment: An analysis of an experimental course in undergraduate moral education using Lawrence Kohlberg's theory of moral development. Unpublished Doctoral Thesis. Cambridge: Harvard University.

Chickering, A. (1969). *Education and identity*. San Francisco: Jossey-Bass.

Dalton, J. C., Healy, M. A., & Barnett, D. C. (1982). Educational approaches to values development in college students: A survey of NASPA chief student personnel administrators. *NASPA journal*, vol. 20, #1, summer.

Erikson, E. (1968). *Identity: Youth and crisis*. New York: W. W. Norton and Company.

Gilligan, C. (1982). *In another voice*. Cambridge: Harvard University Press.

Heath, D. (1968). *Growing up in college*. San Francisco: Jossey-Bass.

Hersh, R. H., Miller, J. P. & Fielding, G. D. (Eds.) (1980). *Models of moral education: An appraisal*. Longman, Inc.

Kohlberg, L. (1975). Moral education for a society in moral transition. *Educational leadership*, vol. 33, #1.

Levine, A. (1980). *When dreams and heroes died*. San Francisco: Jossey-Bass.

Lickona, T. (1976). *Moral development and behavior: Theory, research, and social issues*. New York: Holt, Reinhart, and Winston.

Mattox, B. A. (1975). *Getting it together: Dilemmas for the classroom*. San Diego: Pennant Press.

Mentkowski, M. (1980). Creating a mindset for evaluating a liberal arts curriculum that has valuing as a major outcome. In L. Kuhmerker, et al. (Eds.) *Evaluating moral development and programs with a value dimension*. Character Research Press.

Meyer, J. (Ed.) (1976). *Reflections of values education*. Waterloo, Ontario: Wilfrid Laurier Press.

Morrill, R. L. (1980). *Teaching values in college*. San Francisco: Jossey-Bass.

Mosher, R. L. & Sprinthall, N. A. (1975). Psychological education: A means to promote personal development during adolescence. *The counseling psychologist*, vol. 2, #4.

Newcomb, T. M. (1979). Student peer-group influences. In Sanford, N. and Axelrod, J. (Eds.) *College and character*. Berkeley: Montaigne.

Perry, W. (1970). *Forms of intellectual and ethical development during the college years*. New York: Holt, Reinhart, and Winston.

Resnikoff, A. & Jennings, J. S. (1980). Influences on freshmen: Intensive case study design. In J. M. Whiteley, et al. *Character development in college students*, vol. 1. Schenectady, New York: Character Research Press.

Rest, J. R. (1979). *Development in judging moral issues*. University of Minnesota Press.

Rokeach, M. (1975). Toward a philosophy of value education. In J. R. Meyer et al. (Eds.) *Values education.* Waterloo, Ontario: Wilfrid Laurier University Press.

Sanford, N. & Axelrod, J. (Eds.) (1979). *College and character.* Berkeley: Montaigne, Inc.

Selman, R. (1976). A developmental approach to interpersonal and moral awareness in young children: Some theoretical and educational implications of levels of social perspective-taking. In John Meyer, et al. (Eds.) *Values education.* Waterloo, Ontario: Wilfrid Laurier Press.

Smith, D. & Peterson, J. A. (1977). Counseling and values in a time perspective. *Personnel and guidance journal,* vol. 55, #6.

Sprinthall, N. A. & Mosher, R. (Eds.) (1978). *Value development . . . as the aim of education.* Schenectady, New York: Character Research Press.

Whiteley, John M. (1982). *Character Development in College Students.* Schenectady, New York: Character Research Press.

CHAPTER FIVE

Planning a Comprehensive Values Education Program

by Jon C. Dalton, Margaret A. Healy, and James E. Moore

The authors' (Dalton, Barnett and Healy, 1982) survey of values education activities revealed that student affairs professionals do a great many things to promote values in college students' development. While there is no shortage of values education activities on most campuses, there is little agreement in the manner in which they seek to promote values development. There is often a lack of educational design and effective planning and coordination in the sponsorship of values education activities. What results is a "patchwork" of isolated activities which share little in the way of common student development goals and outcomes. If promoting values is to be an important goal of student development, it is clear that a more systematic and intentional approach to values education is needed.

While no single educational strategy can work in all colleges and universities because of their great diversity of mission and organization, it is possible to identify some educational approaches that have been frequently used and researched extensively. In this chapter we will describe a programming model which can be used for planning and evaluating values education activities. This model should prove useful not only in suggesting specific program strategies and activities but also in demonstrating how such student development interventions fit into a comprehensive program of values education.

The three important components of this programming model are: *approaches, methods, and activities.*

1. Approach

A values education "approach" is the particular educational strategy used to promote values development. Knowing something about the educational approach helps us to understand the intended goals and outcomes of values education interventions. In essence, the educational approach answers the question of *why* values education is conducted. Four approaches will be presented and used as a framework for categorizing the most popular values education activities currently used by college student personnel staff.

2. Method

A values education "method" refers to the specific type of educational intervention used when conducting values education activities. Three methods are used to classify values education activities and interventions. These three methods are: instruction, consultation, and administration. These methods help us to understand *how* values education is conducted. The values education methods are based on the student development intervention models developed by Miller and Prince (1976) as well as the model of program intervention proposed by Hurst, Morrill and Oetting (1980).

3. Activity

A values education "activity" represents a specific educational intervention which is used to promote values development in students. These activities demonstrate the content of values education or *what* it concerns.

In the next section, we will discuss the four values education approaches, the three methods, and illustrate some of the types of values education activities used with these approaches and methods. We will show how a planning model utilizing the approaches and methods can be used to develop a comprehensive values education program.

Values Education Approaches

1. Values Transmission

Transmission is probably the most extensively used approach in values education since it is both consciously and unconsciously applied (Superka, 1976). The purpose of the transmission approach is to instill or inculcate in students certain values which are considered important or desirable. In the transmission approach, values are regarded as standards or rules of behavior which come from society. With the transmission approach, students are generally treated as reactors rather than initiators. The emphasis in the transmission approach is upon conveying values which are believed to be vital to society and indispensable to youth who are being trained to assume roles prescribed by society.

Historically, transmission was the earliest values education approach used in American higher education. Throughout almost all of the 19th century the most important course in the college curriculum was moral philosophy which was often taught by the college president. It was regarded as the capstone of education and its purpose was to help students place knowledge within the framework of a set of values (Hastings Center, 1980). These values were transmitted directly to students because such values were regarded as indispensable for the educated person.

2. Values Clarification

The clarification approach was popularized in the 1970s chiefly by Simon (1972), Raths (1966), Kirschenbaum (1977), and Harmin (1973). The central focus of this approach is to help students use rational thinking and emotional awareness to clarify personal values. Clarification is quite different from transmission since there is a conscious effort to avoid direct inculcation of values. Students are encouraged to become aware of their own values through a process of self-examination and reflection. The clarification approach has a *value-neutral* orientation and does not seek to transmit any particular values as preferable to others nor is it prescriptive about how individuals should act. While the transmission approach relies heavily on external influences to promote values development, the clarification approach relies on the internal processes of self-reflection and awareness. This latter feature makes the clarification approach especially attractive in situations where there is concern to avoid the appearance of indoctrination of values. Values clarification has been popular among student development educators for this reason. It has been criticized, however, for its implicit relativism with respect to values and for conveying "hidden" values.

3. Moral Development

The newest of the values education approaches is the moral development or moral reasoning approach. This approach has received considerable attention in recent years because of the research of Kohlberg (1969, 1973, 1979), Sprinthall (1978), Lickona (1980), Rest (1979), Perry (1970), and others. The moral development approach attempts to stimulate students to think about moral issues and to use reason to examine the implications of moral problems in order to promote higher stages of moral development. Kohlberg's research, in particular, demonstrates that individuals are stimulated to develop increasingly sophisticated levels of moral judgment as they engage in thoughtful consideration of moral issues. This approach has generally been well received by educators because its emphasis upon cognitive analysis and development "fits" in the academic setting. Like the transmission approach, it regards certain moral values to be preferable to others but shares with the clarification approach the conviction that values can only be developed through thoughtful analysis and self-examination. In this respect the moral development approach integrates the social and personal dimensions of ethical development.

4. Moral Action

The fourth values education approach is probably most unlike the other three. It does not emphasize reasoning, nor does it attempt to inculcate values directly or to establish some values as preferable to others. Rather, this approach is based on the conviction that values are internalized only as an individual moves beyond thinking and feeling to action. Consequently, the critical factor in this values education approach is the experience of real life situations in which there is an active interplay between choices and actions. Unlike the transmission or clarification approach, the source of values is neither primarily external nor internal, but in the interaction between the two. The moral action approach stresses the importance of putting convictions into action in the belief that values are never internalized until they have been confirmed in experience.

Values Education Methods

There are generally three types of educational intervention used for values education. While the values education approaches provide a framework of goals and objectives for values education, the three educational methods provide practical strategies for values education interventions. The three methods are both comprehensive (almost all types of values education interventions can be grouped according to the three methods), and practical (the three methods provide useful strategies for addressing values education issues). These three methods of values education are:

1. Instruction

The instruction method of values education includes both formal classroom instruction and informal activities designed to convey information about values and the valuing process to students. The instruction method is usually designed to give students knowledge as well as an opportunity to apply the knowledge in their own personal lives. Although student affairs staff frequently use classroom settings for values education instruction, they are more often involved in values education instruction through workshops, training programs, and noncredit classes. Alcohol education, leadership training, career exploration, and values clarification are some examples of popular co-curricular values education activities conducted by student affairs staff.

The instructional method may be content or process oriented. Some student affairs staff are engaged in teaching *about* values to students or in attempting to convey values directly to students. Others focus on the *process* in which values are acquired and how they influence behavior. In the first instance, the object of instruction is to convey specific values content to students; in the second, the educational objective is to educate students about the role which values play in personal conduct and action.

Another defining characteristic of the instruction method is that it is typically used for values education activities with *groups*. Whether it is a class, a student organization, a group of student leaders, or an ad hoc group of students, the instruction method is typically used for group educational activities. Consequently, it is probably the most frequent method used by student affairs staff for values educational activities.

2. Consultation

The consultation method of values education involves a voluntary relationship in which the student affairs staff member provides assistance to individual students or student groups (Miller and Prince, 1976). Activities such as counseling, advising, and role-modeling are good examples of the consultation method which have important values education uses. The goal of the consultation method is to assist students to be able to decide for themselves what are appropriate personal value commitments. Although the consultation method is often used with groups, it is perhaps most effective in one-to-one interactions where there is personal communication and interaction.

Consultative relationships with staff can be highly influential in helping students to clarify their own values and to commit themselves to a personal set of values. One important reason for this may be that most college students are in a developmental period of establishing independence and autonomy and are more receptive to information and assistance they seek out as opposed to information "laid upon'" them by others, particularly those whom they regard as authority figures.

3. Administration

Administration of the rules, procedures, and physical and human resources of a college or university can also be a very influential method of promoting values among college students.

The role of monitoring the environment is often called milieu management; however, "administration" is probably a more familiar and practical term for student affairs staff. Student affairs staff frequently have responsibility for administering student conduct rules, institutional policies as well as physical facilities, and staff (very often including students). Administration inherently involves the interpretation of rules and policies and the exercise of power and authority and decisions about what is appropriate and inappropriate in student conduct. Consequently, administration typically uses a values transmission approach since it is primarily concerned with conveying certain values or standards which are viewed as essential to community life.

While many student affairs staff are actively involved in promulgating and enforcing such rules, they often do not recognize the fact that such activity constitutes a powerful values transmission role. Those who do recognize this circumstance often experience a conflict with their desire to be nonjudgmental and value-neutral, on one hand, and their obligation to directly transmit values and conduct standards on the other. The more administrative responsibility one takes on, the more intense this dilemma can become. This is one reason, perhaps, why young professionals so often regard senior administrators as conservative and traditional on value issues. It is not only a reflection of difference in age but, more importantly, of role. Most young professionals typically have less administrative duties and, therefore, do not have a significant responsibility for defining and conveying community values and standards.

Whether or not student affairs staff recognize their role in transmitting values, students seldom fail to recognize it. Perhaps more than any other role, the administration of rules and regulations defines the moral style of student affairs staff for most students.

As student affairs staff perform administrative tasks, they are directly and indirectly engaged in tasks which have important influences on value development in college students. Research (Whiteley, 1982; Purple and Ryan, 1976; Miller and Prince, 1976), has shown that environmental factors can have a powerful impact upon college student development and it is important to see administration as a significant method for shaping the milieu so as to promote value development in students.

If instruction is typically used with groups and consultation with individuals, it is possible to view administration as a method of shaping the college social and physical environment in which groups and individuals interact. Consequently, the method of administration can be used to influence values among both groups and individuals. The impact of administration on value development in students should be consistent with the educational goals of instruction and consultation. If, for example, student affairs staff sponsor values education programs on tolerance and nondiscrimination while there is little commitment to these value outcomes in the administration of college rules and regulations, then the educational effect will obviously be limited.

A Model for Planning and Assessing Values Education Activities

In order to create an environment in which students are exposed to value issues and in which their ethical development is promoted, it is best to utilize all of the values education approaches and methods we have described above. A values education program that focuses entirely on *transmitting* values through such activities as ethics classes, Bible study, or chapel services will have a limited impact only upon students. Some students are turned off by approaches which seek to inculcate values directly. They may, however, be more receptive to values clarification activities in which the emphasis is upon the discovery of one's own values and how those values influence personal decisions and moral choices. Indeed, some students may have little direct interest in *talking* about values at all but may be very responsive to the opportunity of working to solve social problems or to help others in need. These opportunities for moral action may serve as a powerful catalyst for moral reflection and development.

Another reason for utilizing all four of the values education approaches is that each of them appeal to different types of individuals and ways of learning. The moral reasoning approach appeals quite naturally to those inclined to examine issues rationally and to *think* and *reflect* on the personal implications of such issues. Other individuals are more oriented to feelings in their response to ethical issues and may be more influenced through activities which touch their emotion. Some individuals, especially during late adolescence, may experience moral issues most profoundly in the context of action in which their thoughts and feelings are tested in real life situations. Consequently, utilizing all of the approaches makes possible a broader values education impact. As Thomas Lickona (1980) argues, morality involves thinking, feeling and behavior, and all must be addressed in values education.

Likewise, all three values education methods should be utilized in order to appeal most effectively to a diversity of individuals and ways of learning. Efforts to promote values education through instructional programs should be complemented by consultation and administrative activities designed to enhance values development in students. Attention should be given to achieving consistency of purpose and outcomes when using different methods of values education.

Values Activities Matrix

The following matrix may be useful both in categorizing current values education activities and in identifying needed areas for new interventions:

VALUES ACTIVITIES MATRIX

SAMPLE ACTIVITIES

APPROACH	METHOD		
	INSTRUCTION	CONSULTATION	ADMINISTRATION

TRANSMISSION	• RELIGION CLASSES
	• CHAPEL
	• ORIENTATION
		• ROLE MODELING
		• ADVISING
		• STUDENT
		  DISCIPLINE
			• CONDUCT RULES
			• POLICIES &
			  PROCEDURES
			• INSTITUTIONAL
			  RULES &
			  REGULATIONS

VALUES
CLARIFICATION
	• ALCOHOL EDUCATION
	• VALUES CLARIFICA-
	  TION ACTIVITIES
	• CAREER DEVELOP-
	  MENT
	• SEXUAL AWARENESS
	• LEADERSHIP
	  TRAINING
		• COUNSELING
		• MEDIATION
		• CLARIFYING
		• TEST INTERPRETA-
		  TION
			• POLICY INTER-
			  PRETATION
			• CAMPUS FORUMS
			• ADVISORY GROUPS
			• FEE REVIEW
			  PROCEDURES

MORAL ACTION	• VOLUNTEER
	  PROGRAMS
	• INTERNSHIPS
	• PRACTICA
	• SOCIAL PROBLEMS
	  CLASSES
		• ROLE MODELING
		• ADVOCACY
			• NON-DISCRIMINA-
			  TION POLICY
			• RESEARCH GUIDE-
			  LINES
			• INVESTMENT POLICY
			• PARTICIPATORY
			  GOVERNANCE

MORAL REASONING	• ETHICS CLASSES
	• USE OF MORAL
	  DILEMMA PROBLEMS
	• ANALYSIS OF MORAL
	  ISSUES IN LITER-
	  ATURE, HISTORY,
	  SOCIAL SCIENCES,
	  ETC.
	• LEADERSHIP
	  TRAINING
		• COUNSELING
		• DISCUSSION OF
		  MORAL ISSUES
		• SOCRATIC DIALOGUE
			• JUDICIAL BOARDS
			• ROOM ASSIGNMENT
			  POLICY
			• BOARD COLLABORA-
			  TION & DISCUS-
			  SION ON POLICY
			  DEVELOPMENT

ACTIVITIES

The values activities matrix identifies 12 categories of activities which can be used in promoting values development in students. Many activities can be used with more than one approach or method as we shall see later. However, some activities are more compatible with particular approaches or methods depending on value objectives and instructional style. Some values education approaches are more suitable in certain educational environments than others and, likewise, some methods may be more effective than others. Staff in private religious colleges may, for example, find it most effective to use a values transmission approach and to concentrate their efforts on integrating values instruction as a formal part of the college curriculum. In public colleges and universities, however, transmitting moral values through instructional activities may violate legal and social requirements for separation of church and state. Consequently, staff in public colleges and universities generally feel much more comfortable with the values clarification approach since it is value neutral and avoids inculcation.

Some values education approaches are more compatible with particular methods than others. The consultation method, for example, is especially compatible with the values clarification approach since both are essentially nondirective in character. The consultation method emphasizes mentoring, counseling, advising, and role modeling, all of which can be highly influential on value development in students but which typically do not involve the direct inculcation of values. Likewise, the instructional method is most compatible with the transmission approach since it usually involves the direct transmission of content from teacher to learner.

An important use of the values activities matrix is to identify those values education activities which are currently used to promote values in student development. Many activities may not be recognized for the significant impact they have in promoting values education in college students. The sample activities included in this matrix are intended to illustrate the uses of the matrix for assessment and planning purposes. Values education activities will vary considerably from campus to campus, and these differences will be reflected in the specific content of each campus values activities matrix.

In this chapter we have attempted to provide a conceptual framework for understanding the variety of educational objectives, pedagogy and interventions used to promote values in college students' development. The values activities matrix can be a useful tool in planning a comprehensive program of values education and in assessing the effectiveness of existing programs.

In the final chapter to follow, James Rest provides a very helpful analysis of the four components of moral behavior and the tasks and complexities involved in evaluating values education programs aimed at promoting moral development.

References

Dalton, J. C., Barnett, D., & Healy, M. A. (1982). Educational approaches to values education: A survey of NASPA chief student personnel administrators. *NASPA journal*, vol. 20, #1.

Harmin, M., Kirschenbaum, H., & Simon, S. (1973). *Clarifying values through subject matter*. Minneapolis: Winston Press.

Hastings Center. (1980). *The teaching of ethics in higher education*. New York.

Hurst, J. C., Morrill, W. H., & Oetting, E. R. (1980). *Dimensions of intervention for student development*. New York: John Wiley.

Kirshenbaum, H. (1977). *Advanced value clarification*. LaJolla, California: University Associates.

Kohlberg, L. (1969). Stage to sequence: The cognitive developmental approach to socialization. In D. Goslin (Ed.) *Handbook for socialization theory and research*. Rand McNally.

Kohlberg, L. (1973). *Standard scoring manual*. Cambridge: Harvard University.

Kohlberg, L., et al. (1979). *Assessing moral stages: A manual*. Cambridge: Center for Moral Education.

Lickona, T. (1976). *Moral Development and behavior: Theory, research and social issues*. New York: Holt, Rinehart, and Winston.

Lickona, T. (1980). Preparing teachers to be moral educators: A neglected duty. In McBee, L. (Ed.) *Rethinking college responsibilities for values*. San Francisco: Jossey-Bass.

Miller, T. & Prince, J. S. (1976). *The future of student affairs*. San Francisco: Jossey-Bass.

Perry, W. (1970). *Forms of intellectual and ethical development in the college years*. New York: Holt, Rinehart, and Winston.

Purple, D. & Ryan, K. (1976). *Moral education: It comes with the territory*. Berkeley: McCutchan Publishing.

Raths, L., Harmon, M., & Simon, S. (1966). *Values and teaching*. Columbus: Charles E. Merrill.

Rest, J. R. (1979). *Development in judging moral issues*. University of Minnesota Press.

Simon, S., Howe, L., & Kirschengaum, H. (1972). *Values clarification*. New York: Howard Hart Publishing.

Sprinthall, N. A. & Mosher, R. A. (Eds.) (1978). *Value development . . . as the aim of education.* Schenectady: Character Research Press.

Superka, D., Aherns, C., Hedstrom, J. E., Ford, L. J. & Johnson, P. L. (1976). *Values education sourcebook.* Boulder: Social Sciences Education Consortium.

Whiteley, J. (1982). *Character development in college students, vol. I: The freshman year.* Schenectady: Character Research Press.

CHAPTER SIX

Evaluating Moral Development

by James R. Rest

Research on the psychology of morality has accelerated within the last decade to the current rate of about 30 books and 200 to 300 published articles and chapters per year (see the annual bibliographies in *Moral Education Forum*, spring issue). Most of this research is dominated by one or another theoretical school of psychology (cognitive developmental, psychoanalytic, or social learning) and, therefore, tends to limit attention to moral reasoning, or empathy and guilt, or to observable behavior. Nevertheless, we are beginning to recognize and understand the complexity of the processes involved in morality and of the multifaceted interconnections among cognition, affect, and behavior. In this article, we propose a framework for viewing the major components of morality and their interrelationships. We believe that any educational intervention aimed at moral development must recognize the multifaceted complexity of the processes involved in morality. Consequently, the assessment of the impact of an educational program upon moral development must take account of the complexities of morality.

We propose that there are four major component processes involved in the production of moral behavior. In other words, a person who behaves morally in a particular situation must have carried out four psychological processes: (1) The person must interpret the particular situation in terms of recognizing who is involved, what lines of action are possible for the actor, and how each of those lines of action would affect the welfare of each party involved. In other words, Component I involves person perception, role taking, imagining consequences of action and how the parties would be affected, as well as constructing mental scenarios of probable causal chains of events set in motion by one's own actions. (2) The person must judge which of the alternative lines of action is more just, or fairer, or morally right. Component II involves assessing the relative strength of competing moral claims, of prioritizing certain considerations above others, of integrating diverse aspects of the case so that a single *moral* directive for action is arrived at. (3) A person is usually also aware that other values besides *moral* goals can be served by alternative courses of action. For instance, one's own personal success or institutional goals may be in conflict with moral values.

While Component II has identified the *moral* line of action, Component III involves actually choosing to do the moral line of action instead of doing other actions that serve other values. Component III involves prioritizing morality above other values. (4) The person must have actually carried through on the decision to do the moral action, persisting and not wandering from the goal, and must have been able to implement that intention. Component IV then involves self-regulation and executive skills to carry out the intention. Each of these processes must have occurred for moral behavior to have occurred. Deficiency in any process would have resulted in failure to act morally. A complete assessment of moral development should determine the developmental status of each of these components.

It is important that attention be given to all four components of morality in designing college student development interventions. As Jon Dalton reports in Chapter Two, much of the values education activities conducted by student affairs professionals is directed at Component I-type concerns: creating awareness and regard for the consequences of certain acts. There is little evidence from this data, however, that sufficient attention is given to other components of moral behavior which involve the commitment and will to act on moral decision. Without promoting such commitment and will, student development interventions may enhance awareness, but do little to promote moral development. The four component model of morality provides both a framework for designing moral development interventions and a means of evaluating their effectiveness.

This model of the psychological processes of morality was derived in the course of reviewing the literature on morality (Rest, 1983) and realizing that different researchers have been investigating different but complementary aspects of morality. The 1983 reference presents a fuller discussion and documentation of this model. Several general points should be mentioned about this model. For one, note that a four-component model of morality denies that moral development or moral decision-making is a single, unitary process. Although one process might interact and influence another process — and although we may find significant correlations among measures of the four processes — still, the four processes have distinctive functions. A student who has great facility on one process is not necessarily adequate on another process. For instance, ability to interpret situations with great sensitivity or the capacity for great empathy (Component I) need not go along with ability to make adequately balanced judgments about what is fair (Component II), nor with prizing justice above other values (Component III). We all know students who can render very sophisticated judgments, but who never follow through on any course of action; or students who have tremendous follow-through and tenacity, but whose judgment is simple-minded. In short, morality cannot be represented as a single variable, nor can moral development be represented as a single set of stages.

As a second general feature of our approach, note that we do not portray the basic elements of morality as being cognition, affect, and behavior. Previous reviewers of morality research have stated that cognitive developmentalists study thinking, psychoanalytic psychologists affect, and social learning psychologists study behavior — as if thinking, affect, and behavior were the basic processes and distinct elements. In contrast, we take the view that there are no cognitions, and no moral behavior that is independent of cognitions and affects. Cognition and affect are inextricably bound in the processes of morality, although for research or theoretical purposes, we can sometimes emphasize one or the other.

Moreover, we view moral behavior as the observable consequence of the four component processes. Since all four component processes co-determine behavior, the correlation of any one of them with behavior may not be high — but it is a mistake to conclude that the processes have nothing to do with behavior.

Third, note that the four components represent the *processes* involved in the production of a moral act, not general *traits* of students. The four components are not presented as four virtues that make up the ideal person, but rather they are the major units of analysis in tracing out how a particular course of action was produced in the context of a particular situation. If a student shows great moral sensitivity in one situation (Component I), it does not necessarily follow that he/she always interprets all situations in this way. If a student uses Stage 4 "Law and Order" reasoning (Component II) in defining the moral ideal in one situation, it does not necessarily follow that he/she will apply that reasoning to all situations. Rather, the four components depict the ensemble of major processes that go into the production of moral behavior in a specific situation.

Note further that we do not intend to convey the impression that the four components depict a linear sequence in real time — that is, that a microanalysis would show that first a person executes Component I, followed in turn by II, III, and IV. Rather, there is clear evidence that the components are interactive; that Components III and IV influence I and II, as well as vice versa. The four processes are presented in a *logical* sequence, as an analytical framework for depicting what must go on for moral behavior to occur.

Now let us consider each Component in more detail and some of the ways each Component has been assessed and researched.

Component I. Component I, interpreting the situation, involves imagining the possible courses of action in a situation and tracing out the consequences of action in terms of how they affect the welfare of all the parties involved.

Four findings from psychological research stand out in regard to Component I. The first finding is that many people have great difficulty in interpreting even relatively simple situations.

Research on bystander reactions to emergencies shows this. For instance, research by Staub (1978) shows that helping behavior is related to the ambiguity of the situation — if subjects are not clear about what's happening, they don't volunteer to help as much. A second finding is that striking individual differences exist among people in their sensitivity to the needs and welfare of others. For instance, this is shown in social psychological research by Schwartz (1977) on a variable he describes as "Awareness of Consequences." A third finding is that the ability to make inferences about the needs and wants of others — and about how one's actions would affect others — is a developmental phenomenon. With increasing age, people tend to get better in being able to make inferences about others. The vast emerging field of "Social Cognition" is relevant here and documents this point (Selman, 1980; Shantz, 1983). A fourth finding is that a social situation can arouse strong feelings even before extensive cognitive encoding. Feelings can be activated before one fully understands a situation (Zajonc, 1980). For instance, Hoffman (1978) has emphasized the role of empathy in morality, and views the arousal of empathy as a primary response which need not be mediated by complex cognitive operations. Hoffman's account is particularly interesting in suggesting how this primary affective response comes to interact and be modified with cognitive development to produce more complex forms of empathy. The point here, however, is that aroused affects are part of what needs to be interpreted in a situation, and, therefore, are part of Component I processing.

Though several approaches for assessing Component I processes are possible, all have some drawbacks. Several paper-and-pencil assessments purport to measure general sensitivity to the needs of others (Schwartz, 1977). However, these are so general and cover such a wide range of situations that they hardly strike us as optimal for evaluating specific professional contexts. Also, there is no evidence that high scorers on a questionnaire are also highly sensitive in a real-life situation. Several measures of empathy have also been employed but these have the same problems as moral sensitivity measures (Sprinthall, 1976).

Currently, the first author is working along some different

lines with Muriel Bebeau and her colleagues in the School of Dentistry at the University of Minnesota. In trying to develop some Component I assessment techniques to evaluate the school's moral education program, we developed some "radio dramas" of moral dilemmas that occur in dentistry. As the drama unfolds on an audio tape recorder, there comes a point when the listener — a dental student — is asked to jump into the dialogue, assume the place of the dentist on the tape, and carry on as if he or she were actually in that position. The response is recorded, and later the student is intensively questioned: Why did you respond as you did? What issues and conflicts did you see in the dilemma? What did you think the consequences of your position would be? And so on.

We are looking at several things: first, can the student come into the dialogue at all and respond within the time period of ordinary conversation? Some students are so flabbergasted that a lot of time goes by before they can think of anything to say. Responding within the limits of real dialogue time is very difficult. Second, does their explanation take account of all the major issues involved? Typically the rights and needs of some parties are not even considered, much less dealt with fairly. Certain sequences of events and consequences are not anticipated. And some students are so preoccupied with the technical aspects of the case (prescribing the correct bridgework, for instance) that the problem of values is hardly recognized. Third, we identify certain assumptions about the dentist's role that seem to blind the student to the professional's responsibility as a moral agent. This research is in progress, but the general approach illustrates an interesting possibility in assessing Component I processes. We are planning to use these new measures to assess the impact of an ethics curriculum in the School of Dentistry on Component I processes.

*Component II.*Whereas the function of Component I processes is to identify possible courses of action and their consequences, the function of Component II is to identify which course of action is the *moral* action (or the one best satisfying moral ideals). Cognitive developmental research — notably that influenced by Piaget (1932) and Kohlberg (1969) — is primarily dealing with Component II processes. Perhaps the most theoretical contributions of the cognitive developmental approach are (1) that development is characterized in terms of a person's progressive understanding of the purpose, function, and nature of social cooperation, instead of characterizing development in terms of learning more social rules, or being more willing to sacrifice oneself. (2) The lasting effects of social experience are portrayed in terms of increased understanding of the rationale for establishing cooperative arrangements, particularly on how each of the participants in the cooperative system are reciprocating the burdens and benefits of that system. Therefore, the general, long-term impact of particular social experiences is characterized in terms of basic concepts of justice (or "schemes of cooperation.") At first, children become aware of fairly simple schemes of cooperation involving only a few people who know each other through face-to-face encounters, and who reciprocate in concrete, short-term exchanges. Gradually they become aware of more complicated schemes of cooperation, involving long-term, society-wide networks, institutionalized role systems, divisions of labor, and lawmaking and law enforcement systems (see Rest, 1979, for discussion). The various schemes of cooperation (or "justice structure") are called "stages" of moral reasoning, each characterized in terms of its distinctive notion of justice — that is, progressive awareness of the possibilities and requirements for arranging cooperation among successively wider circles of participants. Each stage is viewed as an underlying *general* framework of assumptions about how people ought to act towards each other. (3) There are a finite number of basic "schemes of cooperation." These can be identified and are essentially like Hohlberg's descriptions of the six stages. Furthermore, the stages comprise an ordered sequence such that the latter stages are elaborated from the earlier. (4) When a person is faced with a particular new social situation and is trying to figure out what would be the moral course of action, the person calls from Long Term Memory those general knowledge structures in order to aid in identifying the most important considerations, in order to prioritize the conflicting claims of various people, and in order to judge which course of action best fulfills one's ideal of justice. And so a moral judgment for a particular situation involves assimilating the situation to general social knowledge, represented by the "stages" of moral judgment. Research in the cognitive developmental tradition is summarized in Rest, 1983.

There is not enough space there to describe and contrast the various measures of moral judgment that exist, and the reader is referred to a recent book by Kuhmerker, Mentkowski, and Erickson (1980) for discussions of several methods. Up to now, the most thoroughly validated and extensively used general measure of moral judgment in college-age populations and older has been the Defining Issues Test (DIT). The DIT has been used to evaluate moral education programs in over 50 studies (see review, Schaefli, Rest, & Thoma, in press). One interesting new development is the construction of tests of moral judgment for specific professions and situations: for instance, P. Crisham has constructed a moral judgment test using dilemmas in a nursing setting, and L. Iozzi has used dilemmas about environmental issues.

Component III. Component III involves deciding what one actually intends to do by selecting among competing values. Typically, a person is aware of a number of possible outcomes of different courses of action, each representing different values and activating different motives. And, it is not unusual for nonmoral values to be so strong and attractive that a person chooses a course of action that preempts, or compromises, the moral ideal. For instance, Damon (1977) asked young children how ten candy bars *ought* to be distributed, as rewards for making bracelets. In interviews, the children described various schemes for a fair distribution of rewards, explaining why they thought a particular distribution *ought* to be followed. However, when these same children *actually* were given the ten candy bars to distribute, they deviated from their espoused schemes of fair distribution, and instead gave *themselves* a disproportionate number of candy bars. Thus, the children's espoused moral ideals were compromised by other motives — in this case by desire for those tasty candy bars.

Given that a person is aware of various possible courses of action in a situation, each leading to a different kind of outcome or goal, why then would a person ever choose the moral alternative, especially if it involves sacrificing some personal interest or enduring some hardship? What motivates moral behavior? A large number of answers to this question have been proposed. We will briefly list some of the theories of moral motivation and give references for some of the research carried out in accord with each theory (see Rest, 1983, for more complete discussion):

1. People behave morally because evolution has bred altruism into our genetic inheritance (e.g., Wilson, 1975).

2. "Conscience makes cowards of us all" — that is, shame, guilt, conditioned negative effect, fear of God, etc., motivates morality (e.g., Aronfreed, 1968; Eysenck, 1976).

3. There is no special motivation to be moral; people just respond to reinforcement and/or modeling opportunities and "learn" social behavior (Bandura, 1977; Goldiamond, 1968).

4. Social understanding of how cooperation functions and one's own stake in making it work leads to moral motivation (e.g., Dewey, 1959; Piaget, 1932; "liberal enlightenment").

5. Moral motivation is derived from a sense of awe and self-subjugation to something greater than the self-identification with a crusade, dedication to one's country, or collective reverence for the sacred (e.g., Durkheim, 1961; Erikson, 1958).

6. Empathy is the basis for altruistic motivation (e.g., Hoffman, 1978).

7. The experience of living in just and caring communities can lead to understanding how cooperative communities are possible and can lead to moral commitment (e.g., Rawls, 1971; Kohlberg, 1980).

8. Concern for self integrity and one's identity as a moral agent is what motivates moral action (Blasi, 1982).

These eight theories about moral motivation indicate the diversity of views on the issue. None of these views is supported by very complete or compelling research evidence at this point, and an enormous amount of work needs to be done on this component of morality.

Similarly, assessment procedures for Component III processes are difficult to recommend. Several familiar tests of values do not seem appropriate, e.g., Allport-Vernon-Lindzey Study of Values: Rokeach Values Test. Assessment techniques need to be developed for studying real-life situations and this research is difficult to arrange. Therefore, we have no specific recommendations for instruments to assess Component III at this time.

Component IV. Executing and implementing a plan of action. As popular wisdom advises, good intentions are often a long way from good deeds. Component IV, executing and implementing a plan of action, involves figuring out the sequence of concrete actions, working around impediments and unexpected difficulties, overcoming fatigue and frustration, resisting distractions and other allurements, and keeping sight of the eventual goal. Perseverance, resoluteness, competence, and "character" are virtues of Component IV. Psychologists sometimes refer to these processes as involving "ego strength" or "self-regulation skills." A Biblical term for failures in Component IV processes is "weakness of the flesh." However, firm resolve, perseverance, iron will, strong character, ego strength, and so on can be used for ill or good. Ego strength comes in handy to rob a bank, prepare for a marathon, rehearse for a piano concert, or carry out genocide.

In one study of Stage Four "Law and Order" subjects on Kohlberg's measure, those with high "ego strength" cheated less than Stage Four subjects with low ego strength. Presumably, the former had "the strength of their convictions," whereas the latter had convictions but didn't act on them (Krebs, 1967). Various other lines of research also suggest that a certain inner strength, an ability to mobilize oneself to action, is a factor in moral behavior. D. E. Barrett and M. R. Yarrow (1977) found that social assertiveness was an important component in children's "prosocial" behavior. Perry London (1970) interviewed people who were involved in saving persecuted Jews in Nazi Germany, and was struck by their adventurousness as well as their caring (presumably an attribute somewhat related to Component IV).

Research with young children has described techniques for enhancing persistence in tasks that require effort, for supplying the "oomph" to improve one's follow-through. These techniques for small children are paralleled by the techniques employed for adults in Rational Emotive Therapy.

Research indicates that resoluteness, deliberateness, and task orientation may be deep-seated aspects of personality organization — some people are generally scatter-brained, fickle, and "weak." Nevertheless, an educational program may increase students' ability to carry through on their moral commitments by strengthening and sharpening the skills of Components I, II, and III. A helpful technique might be role-playing simulations in which the student goes through the actual motions of putting a plan into effect and works out exactly what to say and how to say it. Assessment procedures and tests for Component IV skills within the college-age populations are difficult to come by; they face many of the same difficulties as Component III assessments. However, examination of the research studies cited may suggest some ways of measuring "ego strength."

Conclusions. The four component model provides a framework for ordering existing research on moral development, for identifying needed research, and for deriving implications for moral education. It suggests if one is to understand and describe moral development in the wider sense of the four component model, one must broaden assessment to match the complexity of the perceived system. Unfortunately, the four component model requires a much more complicated research enterprise than single variable theories of morality. It entails much more complicated educational interventions strategies as well, if development means building adequate functioning in all four major components. Research on Component II perhaps has more of a head start than research on the other components. However, to clarify its role within moral development, research on the other components must progress. Hopefully, this more complicated picture of moral development will not dissuade research in this area and will lead, instead, to more accurate and powerful models.

References

Aronfreed, J. (1968). *Conduct and conscience.* Academic Press.

Bandura, A. (1977). *Social learning theory.* Englewood Cliffs, NJ: Prentice-Hall.

Barrett, D. E. & Yarrow, M. R. (1977). Prosocial behavior, social inferential ability, and assertiveness in children. *Child development*, 48, 475-481.

Blasi, A. (1982). Moral identity: Its development and role in moral functioning. In W. M. Kurtines and J. L. Gerwirtz (Eds.), *Morality, moral behavior, and moral development.* New York: Wiley.

Damon, W. (1977). *The social world of the child.* San Francisco: Jossey-Bass.

Dewey, J. (1959). *Moral principles in education.* New York: Philosophical library.

Durkheim, E. (1961). *Moral education.* New York: The Free Press.

Erikson, E. (1958). *Young man Luther.* New York: Norton.

Eysenck, H. J. (1976). The biology of morality. In T. Lickona (Ed.), *Moral development and behavior* (pp.198-223). New York: Holt, Rinehart & Winston.

Goldiamond, I. (1968). Moral development: A functional analysis. *Psychology today*, 2 (4), 31-f.

Hoffman, M. L. (1978). Empathy, its development and prosocial implications. In C. Keasey (Ed.), *Nebraska symposium on motivation* (Vol. 25). Lincoln, NE: University of Nebraska Press.

Kohlberg, L. (1969). Stage and sequence: The cognitive-development approach to socialization. In D. Goslin (Ed.), *Handbook of socialization theory and research.* Chicago: Rand McNally.

Kohlberg, L. (1980). High school democracy and educating for a just society. In R. L. Mosher, *Moral education : A first generation of research and development.* New York: Praeger.

Krebs, R. L. (1967). *Some relations between moral judgment, attention, and resistance to temptation.* Unpublished doctoral dissertation, University of Chicago.

Kuhmerker, L. (Ed.) (1975-onwards). *Moral education forum.* Spring Issue.

Kuhmerker, L., Mentkowski, M. & Erickson, V. L. (1980). *Evaluating moral development and evaluating education programs that have a value dimension.* Schenectady, NY: Character Research Press.

London, P. (1970). The rescuers: Motivational hypothesis about Christians who saved Jews from the Nazis. In J. Macaulay & L. Berkowitz (Eds.), *Altruism and helping behavior.* New York: Academic Press.

Masters, J. C. & Santrock, J. W. (1976). Studies in the self-regulation of behavior: Effects of contingent cognitive and affective events. *Developmental psychology*, 12(4), 334-348.

Mischel, W. (1974). Processes in delay of gratification. In L. Berkowitz (Ed.), *Advances in social psychology*, Vol. 7. New York: Academic.

Piaget, J. (1965). *The moral judgment of the child.* [Gabain, trans.] New York: The Free Press. (Originally published, 1932.)

Rawls, J. (1971). *A theory of justice.* Cambridge, MA: Harvard University Press.

Rest, J. R. (1979). *Development in judging moral issues.* Minneapolis, MN: University of Minnesota Press.

Rest, J. R. (1983). Morality. In J. Flavell and E. Markman (Eds.), Cognitive development, Vol. IV, in P. Mussen (General Ed.), *Manual of child psychology.* New York: Wiley.

Schaefli, A., Rest, J. R. & Thoma, S. J. Does moral education improve moral judgment? A meta-analysis of intervention studies using the defining issues test. *Review of educational research*, in press.

Schwartz, S. H. (1977). Normative influences on altruism. In L. Berkowitz (Ed.), *Advances of experimental social psychology*, Vol. 10. New York: Academic Press.

Selman, R. L. (1980). *The growth of interpersonal understanding*. New York: Academic Press.

Shantz, C. U. (1983). Social cognition. In J. H. Flavell and E. M. Markman (Eds.), *Cognitive development*, volume in P. H. Mussen (Ed.), *Manual of child psychology*, 4th edition. New York: Wiley.

Sprinthall, N. A. (1976). Learning psychology by doing psychology: A high curriculum in the psychology of counseling. In G. D. Miller (Ed.), *Developmental education and other emerging alternatives in secondary guidance programs* (pp. 23-43). St. Paul, MN: Minnesota Department of Education.

Staub, E. (1978). *Positive social behavior and morality: Social and personal influences*, Vol. I. New York: Academic Press.

Staub, E. (1979). *Positive social behavior and morality: Socialization and development*, Vol. II. New York: Academic Press.

Wilson, E. O. (1975). *Sociobiology: The new synthesis*. Cambridge, MA: Belkap Press of Harvard University Press.

Zajonc, R. B. (1980). Feeling and thinking: Preferences need no inferences. *American psychologist, 35*, 151-175.

IN CONCLUSION

by Martha McGinty Stodt

The first chapter of this monograph traced the values development that can occur while students attend college and the concern of student personnel administrators with values education historically. The remainder of the monograph chapters focused upon various aspects of values development including its complexity, on approaches to value development, and on specific programs in values education. Perceptions of students about their own development during the college years were presented in one chapter. This concluding note presents one student personnel administrator's personal perspective on the evolution of values in individuals and its relevance to a college education.

Most educators assume that values development is implicit in the educational process and is an inevitable outcome of a general college education, so that nothing need be done about it. However, the view that values development must be actively and consciously fostered in the collegiate experience is controversial. The controversy involves two basic issues: one, the content of value systems; and two, the amount of higher education's scarce resources that should be allocated for values development. Faculty, administrators, governing boards, and the American public have all challenged the appropriateness of values education as a function of higher education.

Since I have sometimes questioned whether colleges should promote values development in students, I have attempted to address the two issues on the basis of my own life experience. My discomfort in the controversy about the content of values education derived from the general tendency to associate values development with religion. It is probably no coincidence that so many early members of our profession moved from the ministry to student personnel work and that a large proportion of our current ranks report that they are actively involved in a religious faith. Some student personnel administrators, however, do not profess a religion and yet we ardently support values education. How did we reach this conviction? For me it was as follows.

Like many of us, I was born into a family with a strong religious affiliation, embracing a theology with the usual accompaniment of prescriptions and prohibitions for behavior. At this stage religious and moral doctrines seemed synonymous. In time, I learned about other religions and I also discovered that few moral beliefs were held universally. The theology and moral code upon which I was reared were no longer absolute to me. In the midst of this relativistic state, however, I learned two things. First, that the absence of absolutes as a guide did not absolve me from making choices about what I believe and how I will conduct myself according to those beliefs. My value system thus emerged. Second, I realized that even though religions and moral codes may be relative, a system of values exists in every human consciousness, whether identified as such or not. Whatever the culture, the social stratum, metaphysical belief, or level of psychological sophistication, values are apparently endemic to human nature.

Concomitantly, I learned to distinguish between stated and operative values. While a young child I observed that believers did not necessarily practice the moral dictums of their religion. I discerned that theology as a metaphysical belief might be separate from the morals as manifested in behavior. It became clear that religious belief and moral behavior could exist quite apart from one another; one could state a firmly held belief, yet act in contradiction to it. I felt guilty when I noticed the inconsistencies between words and behavior of my loved ones and other respected adults. Yet it was necessary for me to work through my disenchantment to a realistic acceptance that "actions speak louder than words." Similarly, I realized that to profess certain values but make choices incongruent with them was self-deceiving and usually dysfunctional.

My own life experiences helped me to resolve my dilemma about whether and how values should be developed in college students. I believe that promoting values development in college students is not only legitimate but also extremely valuable.

Either people will develop their own values or they will inherit them from parents or other external sources. The process of free and open values development requires individuals to face values dilemmas, to discuss values with others for the purposes of clarification and shaping values. For example, if I had not established my own values apart from those of my environment, I would believe that "nigras" are supposed to use the back door and eat in the kitchen, that it violates nature for Jews to marry Gentiles, that dancing and drinking are inherently evil, and that all those who do not embrace a particular theology are condemned. On the other hand, I inherited and retained a preference for honesty over deceit and for gentleness over violence; I experienced the pleasures of helpfulness to others all my life; and I have never found a better dictum than "do unto others as you would have them do unto you." In my judgment, even individuals who adhere to the values of their parents must undergo a process by which they make those beliefs their own. Values development is part of the maturation process that facilitates the development of autonomy, a characteristic that allows people to function more successfully as workers, spouses, parents, and citizens. Conversely, to profess certain values and not act according to them can create many emotional problems and much personal unhappiness — and a pervasive sense of guilt.

With respect to the process and content of values development, I believe that values education should have certain characteristics which have been delineated elsewhere in this document. First, values education should enable students to identify and crystallize their values. If they can become aware of their own premises, they car examine them analytically and empirically and strive to alter them if they choose. Through such awareness, people are better able to monitor the inconsistencies between their behavior and their beliefs. As proposed throughout this monograph, values education should help students to reflect their beliefs in action. Congruence between beliefs and behavior is essential to the integrated personality and the fulfilled life. Values education should also assist students in making the commitments integral to a values system while recognizing that values change in the course of life experiences. Within this context, promoting value development in college students might be expected to produce graduates who would function maximally in the roles required of adults in our society.

Like many of my peers, I must ruefully report that my own college education had little if anything to do with my struggle to clarify and to shape my values. Teachers and staff were remote from anything to do with my life, other than receiving lectures, assignments, and grades from them. I was not offered any opportunity to discuss my values with them. As a result, I struggled long and hard in this important process — perhaps unnecessarily.

Even if the usefulness of values development is established — faculty, legislators or the public might reply: "Why should precious funds be taken from the regular academic curriculum to support special programs in values development? Surely this task lies within the province of the church and the home."

Unquestionably, values development takes place, implicitly and explicitly, within the church and the family. The position taken in this monograph is that neither institution nor both together are adequate for the entire process of values development. Moreover, educational institutions are the logical supplementary settings for two basic reasons: first, they can provide greater objectivity, and second, they contain the diversity that church and home may lack. Churches relinquish objectivity when they adopt faith doctrines; and families by nature are highly subjective, often capricious, and sometimes damaging influences on values. Each agency imposes its view of truth and purpose and prescribes how a member should live. Most schools, on the other hand, are likely to present alternatives and methods by which to evaluate and choose, thus enabling the individual to build his own value system. Similarly, homogeneity in belief and behavior is fostered by the structures and teachings of both family and church; whereas the educational community fosters and extols diversity of beliefs and behaviors among its members. This relatively neutral and varied setting provides the optimum environment for fledglings to try out and strengthen their wings before launching into mature flight.

In view of the assets of the university for values development, how propitious it is that the majority of our students enroll during the years of their most crucial life decisions when choices flow from current developmental tasks and eventually form a value system. For example, note how frequently developmental issues were cited by students in Chapter Three as "character building." Clearly decisions about the kind of person one wants to be, the career one seeks, the lifestyle to which one will aspire, and the relationships one will maintain, strongly influence, if not determine, one's value system. As Erikson (1968) suggests, resolution of identity formation in roles as a worker and as a sexual being culminates in the development of an ideology; conversely, irresolution of identity issues may impede development of a values system in which one's beliefs and behavior are congruent.

Confirmation of Erikson's idea emerged in my own research (1972) of young women entering childhood education, some of whom continued as classroom teachers while others became supervisors, principals and teachers of teachers. In a content analysis of their autobiographies written as young adults upon entering a graduate program in teacher training, those who remained teachers of children had written as "daughters." They were still very involved with their parents and had made no mention of concern with mankind or any statement that indicated a commitment to anything larger than self. On the other hand, the women who later assumed leadership roles had written of conflict and resolution of their parental relationships and described ideological commitments. Erikson (1964) also points out that the refinement of one's value system continues on in adulthood and contributes to "generativity." Unquestionably many of our mature adult students are motivated by the desire to improve their social and economic status but they also wish to lead more productive lives.

In view of the prevalence of crucial life decisions during the college years and their contribution to the development of a value system, these developmental issues would seem to deserve the attention and some of the resources of institutions of higher education. Especially is this true since poor identity formation, faulty career choices and incompetent personal relationships cause painful frustration and defeat — costly both to the individual and to society. Furthermore, anti-social values are more likely to evolve from unfulfilled lives. Yet, as we know, campus services that focus on developmental issues have been "extra-curriculum" at best, have rarely been seen as part of a college's mission and have usually received only minimal resources.

Concomitant with the fiscal stringency of recent years, however, has been a growing recognition of the benefits of meeting students' social and emotional as well as intellectual needs (Astin, 1985). Programs, services and teaching that *involve* students with the college experience and thereby promote persistence through college are receiving sympathetic consideration by both higher education institutions and society. Values education programs should also be viewed from this perspective. Clearly college students are forming their values as they struggle with identity, independence and interdependence, occupational and marital choices, and social issues. Assistance with these vital decisions would not only promote values development but would undoubtedly also involve them more with the educational institution. A crucial aspect of our current values education programs is the extent to which they confront students with real choices. In short, do they focus primarily upon abstract issues or do they require students to apply values to daily decisions upon which they can act? The latter would be much more *involving* because actual choices entail opportunity costs and would have consequences.

Also, since values are not held unless they are reflected in action, one would want to expose students to real choices as the most effective mode of values education. For example, a campus discussion of *triage* as applied to starvation in a remote country becomes a more genuine expression of values if it requires action on the part of the student such as fasting for a day or more in order to send a contribution to Ethiopia. Similarly, one's true operant attitudes toward a racial or ethnic minority are revealed in ratio to the degree of one's social intimacy with that group and the economic parity one accepts. As indicated in Dalton's chapter four, residence hall life is rich with opportunities for examining real issues of privacy, territoriality and cooperation. Even simulations, if they are realistic enough, can be useful for non-residential as well as residential students. Is an unwanted pregnancy or an abortion viewed as an opportunity to thoughtfully consider the issue of responsibility in sexual relationships or only as a "moral" issue? Can we help students to evaluate occupations within the context of their value system as well as from utilitarian perspectives? Values education could be a powerful component of student development if colleges design programs that will assist students with developing their values as they accomplish developmental tasks and are alert to the potential for values development in the daily incidental decisions that faculty and staff face with our students.

Throughout this monograph an assumption has been made that values development will inculcate beliefs and behavior indicative of mature, fulfilled human beings and constructive citizens. Needless to say, persons can develop powerful value systems that are damaging to themselves and to society. A basic premise for values education to me is that it should not indoctrinate but should enable students to explore specific values and their consequences for themselves, others, and society. This process would undoubtedly encourage positive human values in most students.

As indicated in the first chapter, promoting values development in students has been a persistent focus throughout the history of our profession; and its importance in the belief systems of the writers of this monograph must be apparent. In fact, one might safely assume that values are not only central to most student personnel professionals, but also that we are extraordinarily conscious of their significance, both positive and negative, in human existence. Certainly we concern ourselves with the promotion of values more than most members of professions such as law and medicine. As a group, we involve ourselves with students' values operationally, both formally and informally, more than faculty and other administrators in higher education. As student personnel administrators, we are not priests or ministers; but we are a branch of educators who care deeply about the function of values in our lives, our students' lives and the world we inhabit with them. Thus are we fully motivated to promote values development in college students. The purpose of this monograph is to strengthen our efforts and increase their effectiveness.

References

Astin, A. (1985). *Achieving educational excellence.* San Francisco: Jossey-Bass, Inc.
Erikson, E. (1964). *Insight and responsibility.* New York: W. W. Norton and Company.
Erikson, E. (1968). *Identity: Youth and crisis.* New York: W. W. Norton and Company.
Stodt, M. (1972). *Autonomy and complexity in women leaders.* Unpublished doctoral dissertation. Teachers College Columbia University.

ANNOTATED BIBLIOGRAPHY

by James Thorius

Banner, W. A. (1980). **The moral philosopher looks at values education.** *New Directions for Higher Education: Rethinking College Responsibilities for Values, 8,* 9-15. San Francisco: Jossey-Bass.
William James, Kierkegaard, Kant, and Arnold, among others, warrant attention as the responsibilities of colleges for the moral education of students are reassessed. It is suggested that the issue of culture as a moral enterprise is at the heart of the argument.

Bell, M. A. & Eddy, E. D. (1980). **Values education: A student's perspective, an administrator's response.** *New Directions for Higher Education: Rethinking College Responsibilities for Values, 8,* 17-25. San Francisco: Jossey-Bass.
A student leader and an administrator discuss the worth of values education to students of 1980, who are part of an increasingly relativistic, unsettled society in which economic matters have assumed primacy.

Bennett, W. J. (1980). **The teacher, the curriculum, and values education development.** *New Directions for Higher Education: Rethinking College Responsibilities for Values, 8,* 27-34. San Francisco: Jossey-Bass.
The values education movement is crucial to the development of moral discernment and character. The moral development of students requires moral character and discernment in those persons who teach and also in the curriculum that is taught.

Blai, B. (1983). Lifestyles and values of college students: Class-es of 1980-1985. *EDRS*, 21 pages. ED 230 137.
The values and desired lifestyles of college freshmen from the classes of 1980-85 at the University of Michigan are examined. Findings concerning student attitudes about work, marriage, family, success, community involvement, altruism, money, and other areas are reported.

Bok, D. C. (1976). Can ethics be taught? *Change Magazine, 8,* 26-30.
The article points out a lack of attention which has been given to the area of moral education by the higher education community. The assertion is made that courses in moral education can have a positive impact on student abilities to reason about and clarify moral dilemmas.

Brown, P. (Ed.) (1982, Jan.-Feb.). Teaching about values and ethics. *Forum for Liberal education.*
Approaches used by colleges and universities to implement values clarification and inquiry, moral education and development, and normative and applied ethics in the curriculum are examined, along with the way that schools are defining values education in terms of their own students and mission.

Brown, R. D. & Cannon, H. J. (1978). Intentional moral development as an objective of higher education. *Journal of College Student Personnel, 19,* 426-429.
The issue of moral education in higher education is addressed in light of the retreat from the practice of *in loco parentis*. Arguments are presented for a renewed emphasis on moral education. A model for implementing moral and ethical education techniques in higher education is presented.

Collier, G., Tomlinson, D., & Wilson, J. (1974). *Values and Moral Development in Higher Education.* New York: Wiley.
This book contains a collection of papers which address a variety of topics pertinent to moral development throughout the curriculum. Information is provided which gives disciplinary perspective for moral development. Contributions of specific subject areas are highlighted.

Conrad, C. F. & Wyer, J. C. (1982, Jan.-Feb.). Seven friends in liberal learning. *AGB Reports, 24,* 10-14.
Liberal arts trends include: a return to the core curriculum, focus on outcomes, emphasis on process over content, interest in the whole student, moral education, a new relationship with the professions in undergraduate study, and new degree forms and delivery systems.

Churchill, L. R. (1982, May-June). The teaching of ethics and moral values in teaching. Some contemporary confusion. *Journal of Higher Education, 53,* 296-306.
Ethical and moral values are taught, and must be, in the sense that they permeate teacher/student relationships and the ethos, methods, and objectives of the classroom. An urgent issue is what values are taught and what theory of education will be rich enough to reflect this practice.

Dalton, J. C. (1977, Oct.). Student development from a values education perspective. *Counseling and Values, 22,* 35-40.
The neglect of values education in the practice of student personnel work is discussed. Three goals of values education are related to the student development concept of integrity. A case is made for the use of values education approaches in the practice of student development work.

Dalton, J. C., Barnett, D. C. & Healy, M. A. (1982, Summer). Ethical issues and values in student development: A survey of NASPA chief student personnel officers. *NASPA Journal, 20, (1),* 14-21.
Report of a survey of chief student personnel officers regarding their perception of the level of importance of values education on their respective campuses. Results provide information about the levels of importance for differing types of issues affecting values development and also who should be responsible for values education on the campus. The results suggest a high level of concern by the chief student affairs officers surveyed that values education is and should continue to be an important agenda item for student personnel work.

Doyle, D. P. (1980, Winter). Education and values: A consideration. *College Board Review,* 15-17.

The relationship between the decline of value-centered education in the 1960s and 1970s and the decline of academic standards is discussed. The question of moral dimensions of learning and how values and transfer of knowledge are irrevocably linked are explored.

Duffy, J. P. (1982, Oct.). Service programs: Do they make a difference? *Momentum*, 33-35.
Comparison of pre and post DIT scores for students involved in service projects is made with a control group of students not involved in service projects. Statistical significance is achieved in gain on the Principled Morality scale for students involved in service project experiences. No such gain is shown for the control group.

Earley, M. et al. (1980). Valuing at Alverno: The valuing process in liberal education. *Department of H.E.W.*, Washington. ED 208 694.
A project at Alverno College that focuses on the way liberal education can enhance the undergraduate student's growth in ethical perception, moral reasoning, and related abilities, is described. Examples of how the curriculum has been rethought and reshaped are presented, and the approaches of instructors in various disciplines to examining the valuing dimension and to implementing challenging teaching/learning strategies are considered. Detailed examples of assessment techniques are presented.

Finches, C. (1980). Values education: A summing up and a forecast. *New Directions for Higher Education: Rethinking College Responsibilities for Values, 8*, 81-11. San Francisco: Jossey-Bass.
Efforts to deal with a continuing crisis in sociological values must involve the best that education, the humanities, and the behavioral sciences can offer.

Gilligan, C. (1982). *In a Different Voice: Psychological Theory and Women's Development.* Cambridge, Mass: Harvard University Press.
Gilligan reports on research which analyzes the differences in moral development of men and women. Documentation

of sex differences is provided. The author argues that these differences have been consistently distorted by theories of human development. Case studies are used to illustrate differences for moral development in men and women. Male-moral development is tied to issues of logic and justice, female-moral development is tied to issues of responsibility for and taking care of others.

Gorman, Margaret et al. (1982). Service experiences and the moral development of college students. *EDRS*, 21 pages. ED 223 173.
The development of moral judgment of students was studied in two types of college courses requiring readings, lectures, and discussions. One of the courses added a component of service to disadvantaged people as a course requirement. Students were pre- and post-tested with Rest's DIT. Those students participating in the course with the service component displayed significant gains in the DIT. Those students participating in the more traditional lecture format did not display any significant change in DIT scores.

Hall, R. T. (1979). Moral education: A handbook for teachers. Insight and practical strategies for helping adolescents to become more caring, thoughtful and responsible persons. *National Endowment for the Humanities*, Washington, D.C., ED 187 617.
This handbook contains background readings, teaching strategies, and units of study for teaching moral education at the elementary, secondary, and adult levels. It offers practical strategies and insights for helping adolescents become more caring, thoughtful, and responsible persons.

Hanson, G. R. (Ed.) (1982). *Measuring Student Development, New Directions for Student Services*. San Francisco: Jossey-Bass.
This volume examines what is known about the measurement of student development. Questions of why and how student development is measured are addressed. A review of available assessment instruments is provided.

Hastings Center. (1980). *The Teaching of Ethics in Higher Education*, New York, 1.

The state of ethics teaching at the undergraduate and professional school levels is examined. The report explores the number and extent of courses in ethics, the status and quality of present ethics teaching, both general and specific problems raised by attempts to introduce ethics into the curriculum, and the steps needed in order to improve the teaching of ethics in higher education.

Hennessy, T. C. (1976). *Values and Moral Development.* New York: Paulist Press.
The book contains papers presented at the 1975 Institute on Moral and Ethical Issues in Education. It is divided into three sections. The first section provides a philosophical and theoretical background to moral education. The second section deals with programs aimed at promoting moral growth in students and the third section is devoted to an analysis of research in moral education.

Hersh, R. H., Paolitto, D. P., & Reimer, J. (1979). *Promoting Moral Growth from Piaget to Kohlberg.* New York: Longman.
This book provides a clear introduction to the cognitive-developmental approach to moral education of both Piaget and Kohlberg. The theory is presented clearly and concisely. The authors also relate theory to practice through addressing such issues as the teachers role, curriculum construction, and the just-community approach. The book is designed as a beginning point for the reader to move from theory to practice.

Hersh, R. H. et al. (1980). *Models of Moral Education: An Appraisal.* New York: Longman.
This book examines six models of moral education: rationale building, consideration, values clarification, value analysis, cognitive moral development, and social action. Because of the complexity of moral education, no one educational model is sufficient. However, the collective strengths of various models can provide the foundation for a comprehensive program in moral education.

Hesburgh, T. M. (1979). *The Hesburgh Papers: Higher Values in Higher Education.* Andrews & McMeel, Inc.

In this book the president of Notre Dame University responds to the critics who see the teaching of religion and values as a hindrance to institutions of higher learning. The significance of values in education is because wisdom is more than knowledge.

Huntsinger, L. et al. (1980, Spring). The University of the Green Woods. *Journal of Environmental Education,* 19-21.
An undergraduate course is developed yearly by a faculty member and upperclass graduates. An interdisciplinary approach is taken to study wilderness and human values.

King, P. M. et al. (1983). The justification of beliefs in young adults. *Human Development, 26,* 106-116.
A model of reflective judgment is described and empirically tested. The model includes seven sets of assumptions about reality and knowledge and corresponding concepts of intellectual justification. This study supports the claim that developmental changes and the assumptions people use when justifying their beliefs do occur in the young adult years, at least among those enrolled in higher education programs.

King, P. M. & Fields, A. L. (1980). A framework for student development goals to educational opportunity practice. *Journal of College Student Personnel, 21,* 541-548.
Discusses the concept of student development, suggests an organizing framework for categorizing its more specific aspects, and illustrates theory application in educational opportunity programming. Student development programs have been hindered by inadequate definitions of student development concepts and the goals they are designed to achieve.

Kirschenbaum, H. (1979). *Advanced Value Clarification.* LaJolla: University Associates.
This book provides a thorough review of the development of the value clarification approach. Part I explores theory and current research. Part II develops designs for workshops, classes and experiences of varying length. Part III describes how value clarification can be built into curricula,

and Part IV surveys past and present developments and forecasts future developments. A comprehensive appendix and annotated bibliography of value clarification, 1965-1975, is provided.

Kirschenbaum, H. et al. (1975). In defense of values clarification. *Humanistic Educators Network, 1.* ED 121 643.
In this position paper, the authors respond to the frequent criticisms and charges that values clarification is value free, relativistic, superficial, and without a cogent theoretical or research base. The authors examine values clarification theory in an effort to address the areas of concern.

Knefelkamp, L. L., Widick, C. & Parker, C. A. (Eds.) (1978). *New Directions for Student Services: Applying New Developmental Findings, 4.* San Francisco: Jossey-Bass.
This volume presents a succinct review of the major theories of human development. Theories which are reviewed include those of Erikson, Chickering, Perry, Kohlberg, Lovenger and Heath. Attempt is made to help the student development professional translate the theories into practice.

Kohlberg, C. & Mayer, R. (1973). Development as the aim of higher education. *Harvard Educational Review, 42,* 449-496.
The article reviews prominent theories of education and concludes that the cognitive developmental approach provides a reasonable understanding of the education process. The article relates cognitive developmental theory to the major emphasis in educational thought and practice.

Kohlberg, L. (1971). Stages of moral development.In Beck, C. M., Crittenden, B. S., & Sullivan, E. D. (Eds.) *Moral Education.* Toronto: University of Toronto Press.
Kohlberg identifies research supporting this stage theory of moral development. Implications of moral development in the educational process are discussed.

Kohlberg, L. (1981). *The Philosophy of Moral Development, Vol. I.* Cambridge: Harper & Row.
A collection of Kohlberg essays on the topic of moral development, written between 1970-1980. Attention is given to moral stages and the aims of education, the idea of justice,

legal and political issues, and problems beyond justice.

Kuhmerker, L., Mentkowski, M. & Erickson, L. V. (Eds.) (1980).*Evaluating Moral Development and Evaluating Educational Programs that have a Value Dimension.* Schenectady: Character Research Press.

A collection of papers on evaluating moral development and educational programs designed to promote moral development. The book addresses the issues of the construction of assessment procedures that are valid, reliable, and easy to administer. Review is provided of conventional paper and pencil tests such as those developed by Kohlberg and Rest. Also, attention is given to an alternative move towards engaging students in an open-ended dialogue about their own development and the role that educational and other life experiences have played in that development.

Leming, J. S. (1981). Curricular effectiveness in moral/values education: A review of research. *Journal of Moral Education,* 10, 147-164.

Research on the curricular effectiveness of a values clarification approach versus a moral development approach was reviewed from 59 separate studies, 33 focusing on values clarification and 26 on moral development. The conclusion suggests that there is little evidence supporting the effectiveness of values clarification approaches. However, the research base for the moral development approach does provide reason for optimism.

Leming, J. S. (1983). *Contemporary Approaches to Moral Education: An Annotated Bibliography and Guide to Research.* New York: Garland Publishing, Inc.

A comprehensive review of the literature encompassing the topic of moral education. The book is arranged to provide the researcher with quick and easy access to moral education topics with similar themes. Citations and abstracts are provided for in excess of 1800 entries.

Levine, C. (Ed.), & Veatch, R. M. (1982). *Cases in Bioethics.* The Hastings Center Report, New York. ED 225 893.

Case studies of ethical issues based on real events are followed by comments illustrating how people from various ethical traditions and frameworks and from different academic and professional disciplines analyze the issues and work toward a resolution of the conflict posed. Case studies include issue on abortion, population programs, patient-physician relationships, homosexuality, enthanasis, human subjects research, and public policy issues including laetrile, etc.

Lickona, T. (1980). Preparing teachers to be moral educators: A neglected duty. *New Directions for Higher Education: Rethinking College Responsibilities for Values, 8,* 51-64. San Francisco: Jossey-Bass.

Using a developmental learning by doing approach, teacher education must take deliberate steps to help teachers acquire the skills and understanding they need to foster the moral growth of students at all levels.

Lifton, P. D. (1982). Personality correlates of moral reasoning: A preliminary report. *Annual convention of the American Psychological Association,* Washington, D.C.

Although psychologists often disagree over the definition, underlying process, and methodology associated among individuals possessing a similar type of reasoning, personality differences were studied of 100 college sophomores identified as moral by the theories of Kohlberg, Hogan, and Haan. Each student was assessed by self-report and observer personality measures.

McBee, M. L. (1980). The values development dilemma. *New Directions for Higher Education: Rethinking College Responsibilities for Values,* San Francisco: Jossey-Bass, *8,* 1-7.

The failure of higher education to provide moral instruction has been responsible in part for the moral problems of this country. Higher education should assume this responsibility with renewed diligence through formal instruction and by colleges and universities being exemplars of ethical conduct.

McBee, M. L. (1982). Moral development: From direction to dialogue. *NASPA Journal, 20* (1), 30-35.

The article suggests that colleges and universities can and must recapture their credibility as educators in the areas of moral and ethical behavior. One way to accomplish this goal is to involve faculty, students, and administrators in a dialogue on values/moral issues. Several strategies for accomplishing this dialogue are discussed.

Maquire, J. D. (1978, Winter). How universities may respond to the values challenge. *Soundings, 61,* 39-42.
Three ways are suggested that will further develop values education, judging, moral discernment, and value guided action within the higher education setting. Organization of the curriculum to heighten sensitivity to values and enhance dexterity in using them; field study to foster ideas in action; and the environment an example of the college itself and strategies which are outlined.

Middleberg, M. I. (1977). *Moral Education and Student Development During the College Years: A Selected Annotated Bibliography.* ED 146 882.
Various aspects of values education and experimental programs in the subject are collected in this annotated bibliography.

Moran, J. D. (1979, Summer). Higher education and moral choices in the 80's. *Liberal Education,* 266-271.
The need for a college to take a more direct role in the moral education of its students is outlined by the president of Boston College. The current moral crisis in our society should prompt post secondary institutions to adopt as a goal the enabling of students to make decisions of a social and ethical nature.

Morrill, R. L. (1980). *Teaching Values in College.* San Francisco: Jossey-Bass.
What is the place of values education in higher education? Does the study of ethics improve moral character? Is it possible to teach values without indoctrinating students? What are the best methods for developing moral awareness in the classroom and in other settings? And how does the campus environment influence students? In addressing these ques-

tions, a systematic analysis is undertaken of contemporary approaches to teaching ethics and values on campus. A comprehensive program is outlined for developing moral awareness and ethical competence in students within the current framework of liberal and professional studies.

Morrill, W. & Hurst, J. C. (Eds.) (1980). *Dimension of Interventions for Student Development.* New York: Wiley.
The book provides college student personnel workers with a resource for the theoretical base of student development. It also examines the major service areas within the context of that theory and offers a model for assessment for needs, evaluation of programs, and planned programmatic changes as a result of assessment and evaluation. Intervention strategies are suggested for particular service areas which address the general goals of many of the student development theories.

Mosher, R. (1980, Oct.). Moral education: Seven years before the mast. *Educational Leadership, 38,* 12-15.
A summary of what is known today about moral education and a suggested agenda for the future.

Paterson, R. W. K. (1979). *Values, Education, and the Adult.* Boston: Routledge and Kegan Paul.
A discussion of the goals of moral education with adult students is provided. The dimensions of moral autonomy, moral awareness, and the ability to make reasoned and perceptive moral judgments are presented.

Pellino, G. R. (1977, Oct.). Student development and values education. *Counseling and Values, 22,* 41-51.
The theories of Kohlberg and Perry are compared and contrasted. Use of these theories in the study of moral development in young adults is discussed.

Raymond, R. C. (1983, Spring). The role of composition in values education. *Teaching English in the Two-Year College,* 199-204.
The article uses material from *Morrill's Teaching Values in College* to assert that teaching can directly address the objec-

tive of values development across the curriculum. Eight components of values education are described. Practical strategies for addressing each of the components of the values development process in the composition classroom are included.

Read, J. (1980). **Alverno's college-wide approach to the development of valuing.** *New Directions for Higher Education: Rethinking College Responsibilities for Values, 8,* 71-79. San Francisco: Jossey-Bass.

This field report from a Catholic liberal arts college for women suggests that, in any environment, a holistic approach to moral development is possible by challenging students to integrate their knowledge with their actions and to deal with inherent values issues both in and out of the curriculum.

Rest, J. (1974). **The cognitive developmental approach to morality: The state of the art.** *Counseling and Values, 18,* 64-78.

Presents a review of the literature relating to the cognitive developmental approach to morality and addresses itself to several questions raised by moral development research.

Rokeach, M. (1975). **Toward a philosophy of value education.** **In Meyer, J. R. et al. (Eds.)** *Values Education.* Waterloo Ontario: Wilfrid Laurier University Press.

The issue of whether or not values education can and/or should remain values free is presented. The case is made that the educators are not fulfilling their educational functions unless they change student values in given directions.

Sprinthall, N. A., Bertin, B. D. & Whiteley, J. M. (1982, Summer). **Accomplishment after college: A rationale for developmental education.** *NASPA Journal, 20(1),* 36-46.

Research on success or accomplishment after college is explored. Studies suggest that although academic achievement in college is not predictive of accomplishment in later life, psychological maturity does have a significant relationship to accomplishment after college. A case is made for promoting psychological maturity as an important part of the college experience.

Sprinthall, N. & Mosher, R. (Eds.) (1978). *Value Development . . . as the Aim of Education.* Schenectady, New York: Character Research Press.
A review of research which attempts to look at the implications of consciously reintegrating moral/ethical values and pedagogical practice in the educational system. The authors have sought to test their rationale in the classroom in order to distinguish failure from success. Efforts pertaining to teacher training are discussed.

Stanton, C. M. (1978, Jan.-Feb.). A perception-based model for the evaluation of career and value education within the liberal arts. *Journal of Higher Education, 49,* 80-81.
An evaluation model for career and values education programs is described. The characteristics, desired outcome, and implementation procedures of Project Cover (developed at St. Louis University) are detailed.

Straub, C. & Rodger, R. F. (1978). Fostering moral development in college women. *Journal of College Student Personnel, 19,* 430-436.
A report of a project designed to test the effectiveness of utilizing a Kohlbergian teaching model to assist with student growth in cognitive moral reasoning skills.

Suttle, B. B. (1983, Summer). Education's failure in critical reflection. *Community College Review,* 38-43.
The author argues that, far too often, academic courses at the community college level do not invite or encourage students to develop and exercise their ability to reflect critically upon their beliefs and values. Four reasons for not adopting a critical reflection technique are outlined and refuted. The article challenges community college personnel to re-examine their instruction methods and actively pursue the use of Socratic techniques on the campus.

Thomas, R. E., Murrell, P. & Chickering, A. W. (1982). Critical role of value development in student development. *NASPA Journal, 20* (1), 3-13.
The article presents the argument that student personnel services do play a major role in the transmission and devel-

opment of students' values. Six roles for the chief student personnel officer are suggested as important factors in effecting values education on the campus.

Trow, M. (1976). Higher education and moral development. AAUP Bulletin, 62, 20-27.

The assertion is made that faculties and colleges have an impact on the moral development of students through basic issues such as what is taught, how it is taught, and who the teachers are.

Wagschal, H. & Beagle, R. (1980). Changing values and higher education. *EDRS, ED 194 393.*

A transcript of a two-member panel discussion on changing values and higher education. Beagle (Edinboro State College, Pennsylvania) stresses that the key to understanding a person's behavior is to understand their values system. Effort should be directed toward discovering value priorities which people have in common and creating behavior change by pointing out these commonalities. Wagschal (Dawson College, Montreal) suggests a redefinition of the liberal arts tradition and new pedagogy based on values reconstruction.

Wagschel, H. G. (1982). The pedagogy of value-confrontation. *EDRS.* ED 229-056.

This paper describes the basic principles and objectives of an educational approach based on "values confrontation" and evaluates its impact on student values, feelings and behavior. The paper stresses the importance of forming a modern pedagogy concerned with developing rational thinking and deeper personal and social awareness. Assumptions concerning college students, based on insights from anthropological, sociological and developmental psychology studies, are presented. A course entitled "In Search of Value" is outlined.

Whiteley, J. M. (1980). Extracurricular differences on the moral development of college students. *New Directions for Higher Education: Rethinking College Responsibilities for Values, 8,* 45-50. San Francisco: Jossey-Bass.

New approaches to investigate the contribution of extracurricular collegiate life to the moral development of students are described. Living environment is found to have the most impact, according to student perceptions.

Whiteley, J. (1982). *Character Development in College Students, Vol. I.* Schenectady, New York: Character Research Press.
The first in a series of comprehensive reports on the Sierra Project at the University of California, Irvine. This book addresses a concern that postsecondary education is neglecting its responsibility for character education. The study describes the Sierra Project as a comprehensive program which attempts to promote ego development, principled thinking and moral maturity. A description of the developmental intervention strategies and assessment techniques is included.

Whiteley, J. M. et al. (1980). **Research on the development of moral reasoning of college students.** *New Directions for Higher Education: Rethinking College Responsibilities for Values, 8,* 35-44. San Francisco: Jossey-Bass.
Although research on the moral development of college students is in its infancy, recent findings indicate promise for future study and institutional action. The theory of moral development is described from a cognitive developmental perspective. Research on improving thinking about justice and fairness at the college level is examined.

APPENDIX
Ten Sample Values Education Programs

1. Title: Being an Ethical Leader
   Goal: To help student leaders define and practice ethical decisions and ethical actions in their student organizations
   Method: Instruction
   Approach: Values transmission
   Domain: Cognitive, affective
   Values Objective: Fairness, honesty, respect for others
   Group Size: 31-50
   Contact: Campus Activities and programs University of Nebraska Lincoln, NE 68588

2. Title: College 101
   Goal: To help students examine the college environment, their individual values, and the relationship between these two systems
   Method: Instruction
   Approach: Values clarification
   Domain: Cognitive
   Values Objective: Responsibility to self, independence, self-discipline
   Group Size: 51-100
   Time Required: 2 hours per session
   Contact: Dean of the College Marietta College Marietta, OH 45750

3. Title: Moral Issues in Group Work
    Goal: Workshop format uses moral di-
                              lemmas to sensitize students to
                              others' values and moral com-
                              mitments
    Method: Instruction
    Approach: Moral reasoning, values trans-
                              mission
    Domain: Cognitive
    Values Objective: Cooperation, respect for others,
                              self-awareness
    Contact: Office of Campus Activities
                              University of Maryland
                              College Park, MD 20742

4. Title: Salvaging the Century
    Goal: A film/lecture series which ex-
                              plores contemporary moral and
                              ethical issues and examines their
                              implications for life after college
    Method: Instruction
    Approach: Values transmission, moral rea-
                              soning
    Domain: Cognitive, affective, behavioral
    Values Objective: Values awareness/social respon-
                              sibility
    Contact: Student Development and Pro-
                              grams Office
                              University of North Carolina-
                              Greensboro
                              Greensboro, NC 27412

5. Title: Clarifying Values in Roommate
                              Contracting
    Goal: To assist residents in comparing
                              values and lifestyles to develop a
                              cooperative mode for living to-
                              gether
    Method: Instruction
    Approach: Values Clarification

Domain:	Cognitive, affective
Values Objective:	Responsibility for self, cooperation, tolerance
Contact:	Office of Student Development Ohio State University Columbus, OH 43210

6.

Title:	Social Justice Awareness
Goal:	Education and action programs designed to promote awareness and action on contemporary social justice issues
Method:	Consultation, instruction
Approach:	Moral action, moral reasoning
Domain:	Behavioral, cognitive
Values Objective:	Helping others, promoting justice
Contact:	Coordinator of Social Justice Programs Gonzaga University Spokane, WA 99258

7.

Title:	Values Concerns Center
Goal:	Provide student development programs which promote moral awareness and action
Method:	Instruction, consultation, administration
Approach:	Values transmission, moral action, values clarification
Domain:	Affective, behavioral
Values Objective:	Responsibility for self, respect for others, religious commitment
Contact:	Student Affairs University of Minnesota at Waseca Waseca, MN 56093

8.

Title:	VISION
Goal:	To encourage moral action and

	commitment through community service
Method:	Consultation
Approach:	Moral action
Domain:	Behavioral
Values Objective:	Self-awareness, helping others, understanding others
Contact:	Campus Ministry Bellarmine College, Newburg Rd. Louisville, KY 40502

9. Title:

Title:	Intercultural Values and Communication
Goal:	To examine values and beliefs of different campus cultural groups and how these affect cross-cultural communication and understanding
Method:	Instruction
Approach:	Values clarification, values transmission
Domain:	Cognitive
Values Objective:	Understanding others, self-awareness
Contact:	E.O.P. California State University Carson City, CA 90747

10. Title:

Title:	Student Mentoring Project
Goal:	To provide mentoring relationships between faculty and students to share values, beliefs, personal commitments
Method:	Consultation
Approach:	Values clarification, values transmission
Domain:	Cognitive, affective
Values Objective:	Values awareness and development

Contact: Division of Student Life
University of Nebraska-Lincoln
Lincoln, NE 68588